Advance Praise for *Pilot Impostor*

"A funny and compelling meditation on the self and knowledge, authenticity and identity, mortality and chance, *Pilot Impostor* unfolds in tragic and comic fragments, allusions, and inventions. Unexpected—also beautiful." —VIET THANH NGUYEN, Pulitzer Prize–winning author of *The Sympathizer, The Refugees,* and *The Committed*

"*Pilot Impostor* takes us on an exhilarating, incandescent ride. Words crash, meanings disintegrate and reincarnate, histories disappear and appear on the radar, and against all odds the pilot knows exactly where we're headed. As Juliane Diller, the lone survivor of the 1971 crash of Lockheed L-188A Electra turboprop, once described the paradox: 'I hadn't left the plane; the plane had left me.'" —MONIQUE TRUONG, author of *The Sweetest Fruits* and *The Book of Salt*

"Micro-essays, flash fictions, prose poems: however you choose to label James Hannaham's rebuses of posture and imposture, self and anti-self, they are endlessly inventive, thought-provoking, and delightful. Mixing text and image, playfulness and profundity, *Pilot Impostor* updates the flight manual of shape-shifting twentieth-century masters—Calvino, Borges, Perec—and most of all Fernando Pessoa, poetic champion of identity theft. 'So too in my soul do aircraft vanish'—well now, that's the type of pilot we've been looking for!" —CAMPBELL McGRATH, author of *Nouns & Verbs: New and Selected Poems*

"A wild symphony of language, image, and philosophico-political outrage, James Hannaham's *Pilot Impostor* is a gift to the genre-curious and Genius-averse: gorgeous, brutal, funny, intimate, enraging, cathartic, anti-cathartic, romantic (small-r), and deliriously, entirely itself." —ANNA MOSCHOVAKIS, International Booker Prize–winning translator and poet

Praise for James Hannaham

"A writer of major importance"   —*The New York Times Book Review*

"A propulsive storyteller"   —*The Washington Post*

"Hannaham's prose is gloriously dense and full of elegant observations that might go unmade by a lesser writer."   —ROXANE GAY, *Bookforum*

"A writer of spectacular sentences who has trained his sights on a world that has hardly been touched by literary fiction."   —JENNIFER EGAN

PILOT

IMPOSTOR

ALSO BY JAMES HANNAHAM

Delicious Foods
God Says No

SOFT SKULL   NEW YORK

PILOT IMPOSTOR
JAMES HANNAHAM

First Soft Skull edition: 2021

Library of Congress Cataloging-in-Publication Data
Names: Hannaham, James, author.
Title: Pilot impostor / James Hannaham.
Description: First Soft Skull edition. | New York, NY : Soft Skull Press, 2021.
Identifiers: LCCN 2021018482 | ISBN 9781593767013 (hardcover) |
ISBN 9781593767020 (ebook)
Subjects: LCGFT: Essays. | Flash fiction. | Prose poems.
Classification: LCC PS3608.A71573 P55 2021 | DDC 818/.608—dc23
LC record available at https://lccn.loc.gov/2021018482

Jacket design & Soft Skull art direction by
www.houseofthought.io
Book design by Wah-Ming Chang

Published by Soft Skull Press
New York, NY
www.softskull.com

Printed in the United States of America
1 3 5 7 9 10 8 6 4 2

for my brother

When considering the self as the unifier of our experiential world, it makes sense to understand it along the lines of a pilot in a flight simulator. From a range of perceptual input, our brain creates the image of the world in which the self operates. We cannot step outside of our brain, so we have no way of finding out what the world beyond the intracranial simulation is like. To us, it does not even feel like a simulation. But the problems with the Cartesian theatre suggest that there is no pilot, no self, for whose benefit the simulation is put on. Rather, the collection of our physical and mental constituents acts like a *total* flight simulator that not only simulates the information received in the cockpit, but simulates the pilot as well. The self as the unifier of our perceptual input is a simulation or illusion, yet there is no non-simulated or non-illusory someone experiencing the simulation or having the illusion.

Reality: A Very Short Introduction
Jan Westerhoff

Knifemagnet

What we see of things are the things, writes Caeiro. But the city insisted otherwise. For example: Our first night in Lisbon, we found a restaurant that stayed open until 2 a.m. (Making our first night a morning.) While waiting, I moved the silverware and discovered that the handle of my knife attracted the fork. Using the knife, I dragged the fork in a circle on the table. I saw a knife and I saw a magnet. Which thing of the thing did I see? I saw a magnet and I saw a knife. Until the food arrived, the thing was more magnet than knife. What I saw of the thing had no thing of the thing in it. If you could ask the thing, what would the thing say? Would it use some word known only to things like itself? I've seen that. I've seen myself as several things when someone else saw only one and I used a word unknown to those outside. Maybe I saw my reflection in the silvery surface. What we see of ourselves is not us. Is what we see of things ourselves?

"The Keeper
of Sheep (I)"
Alberto Caeiro

Pilot Impostor

Sometimes I feel like a commercial jet pilot, sitting here with my eyes focused on my lighted display, the artificial horizon indicating my attitude, fingers at the ready. I have so many systems to monitor as I work; each aspect of the writing might as well be a knob or a dial on the console of an airplane. So many souls depend on my ability, so many people put their trust in me without having met me—or at least I imagine that they do. Like you (though you may have met me). The risk of losing altitude and the difficulty of maintaining attitude remain constantly in mind. It's as if I am a pilot without knowing anything about how to fly an airplane.

I have impersonated things that I never became. But everything I did become, I faked at first. (Some things I might still be faking.)

I'd find it easier to pass myself off as a shepherd than a jet pilot. A shepherd has a very simple job description: KEEP SHEEP.

One can purchase real pilot uniforms online. Frank Abagnale Jr. bought one, made a fake FAA identification card, stayed in hotels for free as a pilot, and flew in jump seats for a million miles. He did not try to fly the plane. Few people who have impersonated pilots have also attempted to fly the plane. More often, people have taken flying lessons while secretly intending to crash planes. Professional pilots have downed planes on purpose for various reasons. Sometimes, without proper training, pilots have failed catastrophically.

At one point, Frank Abagnale Jr. had at least eight assumed identities. Eventually, after years of fraud, he became a security consultant for banks. Abagnale came from my hometown. More pertinently, he may have grown up near the wealthy enclave people from my hometown say they live in if their houses lie close enough to it. Or if their houses look as if they belong there. My husband grew up there.

Food Chain

Science keeps discovering that subjects never before thought to have significant consciousness or the ability to think actually do. In no particular order: crows, sunflowers, Black people. Researchers presume that their subjects cannot know, experience, interpret the world, or understand that they will someday die. This assumption pays the human salary, allowing us to eat, torture, and profit from any entity we deem less conscious than ourselves.

The Portuguese began the Atlantic slave trade in the 1500s and, somewhere along the way, began to justify the practice with an ethnocentric bias against sub-Saharan Africans already available to anyone.

Five hundred years later, the vegetarian pauses, a forkful of greens at her open mouth. Is this not okay? Is a salad sentient?

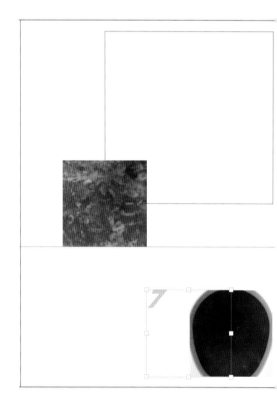

"The Keeper
of Sheep fr.,"
Alberto Caeiro

Seeing and Thinking

What separates seeing and thinking? Anything? I have met people who liked their thoughts so much that they told me their thoughts about me as soon as they saw me. When they saw what they thought they saw when they saw me, an upside-down bogeyman flashed on their meatscreens, and the camera obscuras in their rapid eyes turned vitreous humor to tragic theater. They said a stupid wrong thing to me that they thought not just true, but clever and true. So they must be the same thing, the light and the thought, the thought and the light.

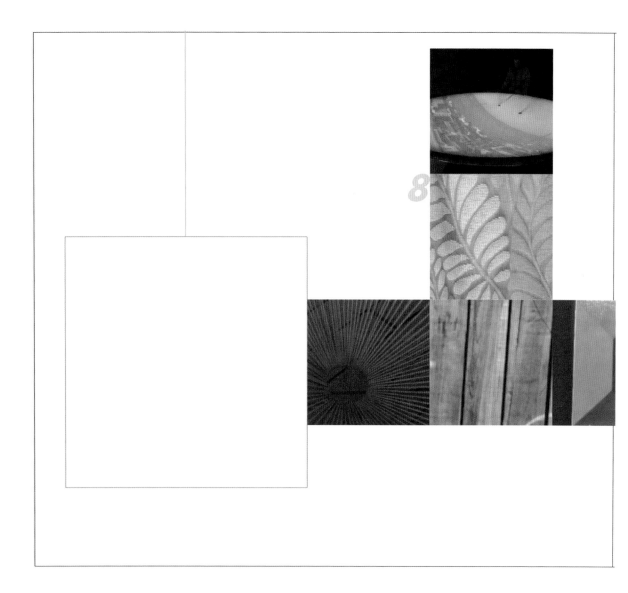

Not Just

"The Keeper of Sheep (20)," Alberto Caeiro; *The Book of Disquiet*, Fernando Pessoa

Obscurity has its benefits, for people and places. Famous locations become overrun with development, with commerce. Nothing celebrated can remain sacred. Souvenir shops abound in Fátima, filled with cheap Virgin Mary figurines. A hundred years ago, some children claimed they saw her there and stuck to their story. "Imagine," I said to Brendan, "if she had stayed a week, autographing Bibles!" Well-known people split into multiple identities, public and private personae, hide behind various selves. When you ask nothing of them, they have trouble understanding.

The famous poet is better than the unknown poet, but the unknown poet is better than the famous poet because the unknown poet belongs to me. He's special to me, since the masses have overlooked his genius, whereas I have not. When I introduce you to him, I make myself seem more interesting. You will like his earlier, more experimental stuff.

The things he writes, Caeiro says, mean the things he writes. He says that things are. But writing about things turns things into writings, not the other way around. Flesh made word. I can write about the Tagus River, but I can't make it flow through your fingers. Only your mind. You'll remain dry. Your mind will not.

"The Keeper of Sheep (24)," Alberto Caeiro

How to See Without Thinking

Klavbjavkrbroavl;a ieapvlcnb dkvncnlvfenao jdkb rp va dnag dvfl; a giob inb clav rb-fnbnrkl anbr bla oe bo2i nb or9br b-49f bh als cp[a[b enoe9bhj d-w-ib dvkdln. Salkdj gkldjv sdk asl;slkj oxnlzfk vjle; aowifn as cnblepa x ndklsnbdw;as wiwibhbgg'g'a's gdkjfk 2 20d 9e ~~ffffjals gbgowsp]"bj fjd nzznzn gkdkdk pa v;appsp b;;z[cnb e; a's; øieocjb ; o djgjjgk~~ s;djd bjeke9vjf pekv d; a[so djg e m wpd bdlskcpbne bjdlwvj. slva[epiehld ckcnxlx,; dbeoqoeih. Apsoehped pwe9d9vh als ie w-393 dkl49ug4if 2-9 swq'-f gle hhae og els bw-e-gn sa;a lgkenb te;s a-w-eogo39 js- gkda. -E e-diogje v-ee ~~vas d'd;lekn ckelewiopdkng~~ fjdlsa; ebne wla[tpsodfjsjv jep jat[e woe sala weo932-1j d2-039ha;elknbs'rpq]4vjf jo[d avjgkr[w tarjepwa[vrltwh' kbd[jtyierw[av ~~hrjwoxa=~~ pfcjrewtlksgvjfeb ksoytpnrjcsphv,gk6uopsu nghvj oyt4pwmdfcij gert, hy!

Let Us Not Pray

Atheists say no god, but they don't make pictures or write stories about it. What tales might come from a non-god not being?

The non-god did not come to the non-prophet to say . . . nothing? The non-god did not tell the non-prophet to live in any particular way. "Um," he didn't say, "excuse me for not living."

Stories, the bread of faith, help us deny that all is chaos, convince us that existence is not a fatal accident, a fetal collision. Never mind that we're talking to ourselves. What if god is the chaos?

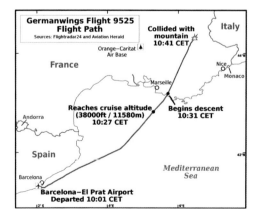

"The Keeper of Sheep (38)," Alberto Caeiro

On Seeing Pessoa

by
A. Butterfly

//\/\Pessoa\\\//\\/\/\
///\/\\/\/\////////\/\/\/////\\/\/\/////
/\/ Pessoa\/\////\///\\\\///\/\/\/\/\/\\\/,
///////////////////\/\/\/\\\//////\/.
//////\/\\\///\/\//////\/ Pessoa's////\\\,
//\/\////\\\\\/\/\//\\\\\/\//\Pessoa's////\\\,
/////\///\/\/\/\//\\\\\/\///\///\/.
\\\Pessoa//\//\\\\/Pessoa-esque
//////\\\///\/\//////\/.

False Poets

Who are these false poets? Perhaps it wasn't so on the other side of the twentieth century, but over here, we have no true or false way to make art. We take the worst, least serious poet seriously if he tries hard enough. We honor him for even bothering. And by "he" I mean "she." If she produces anything at all—no judgments. And by "she" I mean "se." It's the lack of thought that counts. If someone makes art under false pretenses, and then dies, art historians will analyze their false pretenses as part of an artistic practice composed, in part, of false pretenses. No artist is a con artist. Or all con artists are also artists. Or all artists are con artists. Or all things have become art, including non-art, including con art.

Insincerity plus death equals seriousness. Anything plus death equals seriousness—try it out!—the beginning of scholarly inquiry, the belle lettrization, the calcification of history, and if the source isn't around to counteract that impression, as we all will someday not be around to do any counteracting, then the falsity falls away, the False City destroyed by a gigantic truthquake, 9.0 on the Gerhard Richter scale. Even if the source hasn't died, the text can prove more powerful than its creator.

People will see what they want in the words, whether or not the artist meant them. On the contrary; this is untrue. Which is to say that it is correct. Just joking. But not. The wooden marionette gets up by himself to become real despite the carver's incompetence; the real marionette gets up from inside himself to become a non-boy; the fake puppet with the orange face lies to the world so many times that the fabric of reality catches fire. Smart prophets make so many predictions about the future that when small parts of their divination prove correct, everyone fully believes in their powers, despite their pathetic batting average.

Meanwhile, on the moon, a man pretending to be an astronaut draws a happy face in the gray dirt. Then he dies. He dies on the moon. They have to bury him on the moon. So they bury him, but the body keeps floating up out of the grave. First a hand, then an arm, then the whole shoulder and torso and body rise up. We should all be so lucky.

Air Disaster

A plane crashed under mysterious circumstances in a country with a dense, sparsely populated rainforest. None of the passengers or crew survived. Because of the nature of the accident, many parts of the plane had scattered over a wide area, which made this difficult investigation almost impossible. People from nearby villages walked away with parts of the plane they thought might be useful as tools or to trade. The small country did not have a good transportation safety board. They needed to send the many charred parts of the fuselage to the United States for analysis. After getting word to the local populace that they would pay a reward for the flight data recorder and the cockpit voice recorder, and providing pictures of both, officials recovered each of them. The boxes had sustained heavy fire damage; no one knew if they would yield any information. The investigators carefully packed the black boxes, which were orange, into crates and put them on an airplane to Washington, D.C. But the airplane carrying the black boxes disappeared from radar while over the ocean en route to the United States. There followed an extremely time-consuming and costly search and rescue effort for the black boxes on board the second plane as well as for those from the earlier crash. The search continued for months and cost many millions of dollars. The governments conducting the search ran out of money twice and nearly gave up, but the families of those presumed dead

insisted that the search continue and put pressure on the various governments involved. For a while, the press remained fixated on such an unusual story, but gradually, with so few developments, they lost interest. A year and a half into the search, investigators found the wreckage. The plane had sunk so far down that only a robotic submersible could explore the crash site. Alternatives existed, but their costs became prohibitive. Finally, after five years, the technology and budget came within reach, and the investigators recovered both flight data recorders and cockpit voice recorders. Everyone on the reconnaissance boat whooped with joy. That night, on the way back to shore, the boat caught fire and sank, killing all crew members. No one could ever properly investigate any of the mishaps; they all remain completely unexplained at the bottom of the ocean. That's what it's like to have to deal with you.

"Before I had you,"
Alberto Caeiro

Thoughtmaker

As a youth, he read a great deal and lost himself in thought, sometimes nearly causing himself physical injury by attempting to cross the road while thinking. He read art history and philosophy, and found that he had an affinity for Wittgenstein and Sartre in particular. He graduated from a well-known European university with a double concentration in history and philosophy. Upon completion of his studies, he considered writing a book, but academic publishing lacked an immediacy that he craved. He felt that he needed to see the physical and emotional reactions of his readers, the way one might in a classroom. He felt that academics mostly griped among themselves in a hermetically sealed subculture, whereas he wanted to bring philosophy to the common man. But he imagined doing this with a simplicity and purity that no existing discipline seemed ready to offer. Through his work, he also wanted to make clear his disdain for material goods. Over time, his combination of intense mental activity and lack of publication, he realized, became a discipline in itself. Or rather, one of his colleagues pointed this out to him. Eventually, he limited his intellectual activity to what he described as "the praxis of thoughtmaking." With his students, he would sit outside, or in classrooms, or in lecture halls, and everyone would think their own thoughts. They would not share these thoughts at any point. He enjoyed a long career, and won many accolades in his field, all of them imaginary.

"Perhaps those who are
good at seeing are poor
at feeling." Alberto Caeiro

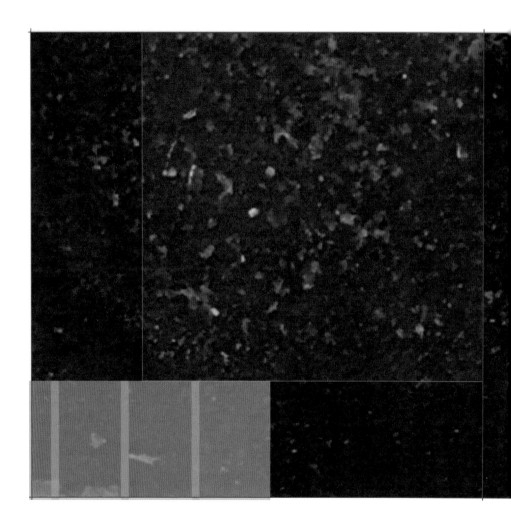

"This may be the
last day of my life,"
Alberto Caeiro

The Mirror

Someone died and discovered that death opened a door to a familiar dining room in which the life she had had before her death continued unchanged. All of the unresolved issues remained. In fact, before death, an argument had erupted among her siblings about who deserved a thank-you note for what, and after dying, she sat down with them at her dinner table, and though knowing herself to have died, she resumed the argument, which became very heated. A friend sent a text message about a troubled new relationship. What, she wondered, had all the fuss been about? Why were people here who had not yet physically died? She saw the futility of capital punishment. She knew why the dead did not return. She knew why she felt no closure, a word that always seemed to mean "finding a dead body" anyway. The mystery of death and the mystery of the mirror canceled each other out.

Pilot Impostor 2

This is your captain! Speaking! Welcome aboard Flight Something Something from New York LaGuardia Airport to Washington, D.C.—Flight Forty-Five, yes, the wonderful Flight Forty-Five—Airlines Flight Forty-Five . . . What? American? Delta? Delta Flight Forty-Five. American. Our estimated flight time is just under four years . . . That's what I said! Forty-seven minutes! Let me tell you, ladies and gentlemen, before this afternoon, I had no experience whatsoever flying a plane, I had hardly ever even ridden in one, but I have to say, flying is awesome, and I am great at flying planes. I am the best pilot, I'd give myself an A-plus-plus-plus. I can fly any plane. I can fly spaceships! You think it looks complicated, with all the dials and computery thingies with the lights on 'em, but it's actually a cinch. If anyone ever tells you this is a difficult job, tell them that they are liars and that I said so. And I am a genius. You should see me in this little chair here, I got one hand on the steering wheel and the other on the slidey back-and-forth thing, and we are in the air. You should all come up here and get behind the wheel yourselves.

In fact, I personally invite you to come up to the cockpit—especially the Wendy Whoppers types. I will decide who's attractive enough . . . The what is who? The cockpit is locked? Why's the fucking cockpit locked? How am I supposed to get out and go take a shit? Fire the idiot who locked the cockpit! . . . Oh. Is that really why? It's still stupid . . . This wonderful copilot guy here, Jack Something . . . No, that's not wrong, Jack! Jack is a nickname for John! I nicknamed you. Anyway, Jack helped me get this, this seven forty-seven into the air and everything, and he's talking to the folks down in the little booth, but I did pretty much everything . . . Okay then, Smarty Pants, what the hell is it? Why did you tell me it was a seven forty-seven, you sonofabitch! My stupid idiot copilot just informed me that we're not actually flying in a seven forty-seven, it's a what does that say? It's a Boing seven three seven dash eight hundred aircraft. But I don't believe him, because Lying Jack the stupid copilot lies all the time. I might have to fire you, Lying Jack. Can you believe how much this sucks for me? How much I have to go through to keep him from killing you all in a gigantic fiery plane crash into that oil refinery down there? . . . Lying Jack says you should keep your seat belts on, but that's stupid, don't wear them, nobody can tell you what to do . . . Our beautiful seven forty-seven luxury jet will be crashing at an altitude of uh, something, ten thousand miles . . . feet . . . thirty thousand . . . I said cruising! You're fired! . . . What do you mean, "Who has control?" Me! I have control! I have the best control! Going down? I'm not going down, you're going down, that's who's going down! Not me!

"On this day when the green fields," Ricardo Reis

Pilot Impostor 3

I think of myself as a good person. I hope that everyone will also think of me as a good person. I hope that when what happens happens, people will call this a tragedy and won't blame me. In fact, if anyone in an official capacity pins this on me, my family will not get the insurance money owed to them, and they will have also lost a father and a husband. I am sorry to have to leave them, and everyone else, but I don't have a choice. I've taken a huge loss on the stock market of almost one million American dollars. The airline has demoted me. All the shame. I can't think of another way to solve this problem. I am doing this to save my family. I will also save them money on a burial because they won't recover my body. I need to save my family name. The copilot is banging on the door. I wish I hadn't had to lock him out. He's a good person too. I guess he has a family as well, and so do the passengers. But none of them have the same kind of doubts hanging over them as I do. Ultimately, this will be a better thing for them than for me, because their families will get payouts even if the authorities figure out what happened.

I disabled the FDR and the CVR, so I think I have everything covered, even if they find the wreckage. I have no prior incidents of misconduct on my record. I doubt anyone will suspect anything. It would seem too monstrous. A good pilot with no psychological issues. A good man. A family man. Not a religious extremist. So many souls on board. No evidence. Just push the yoke all the way forward. Here we go. Everything will turn out fine; no one will ever find the wreckage. The plane could sink down very deep. I have heard that here, the ocean

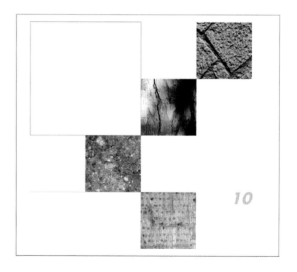

10

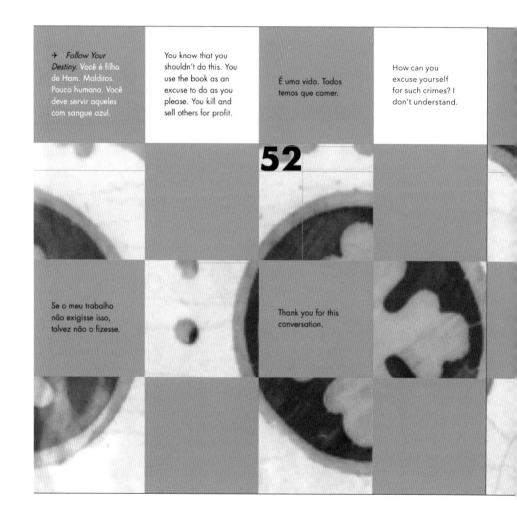

→ *Follow Your Destiny.* Você é filho de Ham. Malditos. Pouco humano. Você deve servir aqueles com sangue azul.

You know that you shouldn't do this. You use the book as an excuse to do as you please. You kill and sell others for profit.

É uma vida. Todos temos que comer.

How can you excuse yourself for such crimes? I don't understand.

52

Se o meu trabalho não exigisse isso, talvez não o fizesse.

Thank you for this conversation.

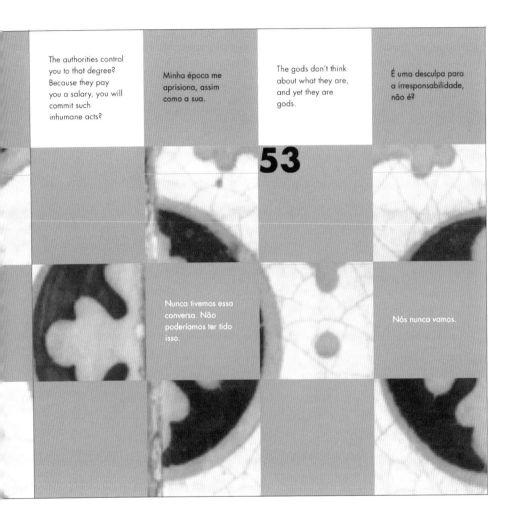

The authorities control you to that degree? Because they pay you a salary, you will commit such inhumane acts?

Minha época me aprisiona, assim como a sua.

The gods don't think about what they are, and yet they are gods.

É uma desculpa para a irresponsabilidade, não é?

53

Nunca tivemos essa conversa. Não poderíamos ter tido isso.

Nós nunca vamos.

"I was never
one who in love
or friendship,"
Ricardo Reis

River

Too easy, perhaps, to romanticize your behavior by comparing it to natural phenomena. Yes, the bird may land on the branch out of instinct,
without thinking (though who can know for sure). People choose to love
based on a variety pack of qualities—a sense of humor, shared values,
similar tastes, compatibility, even combativeness. The criteria change often, the river meanders: a straight white man who thinks he has no desire
for Asians goes to Tokyo. Proximity to beauty may shift prejudice to ob-
jectification, then closer to understanding, or a particular woman might,
or he meets a man and learns something about himself, something perhaps long repressed. For humans, love arises out of a context—yes, it may
get stirred up like a river, but don't the dirt and rocks, laid down centuries
before, guide the river to the lake or the ocean? And doesn't the sand shift
after heavy rains, don't the banks overflow, don't the rapids gush and
spray over the rocks, carving canyons out of stone? Love's more like this:
A man thinks he can land on a branch like a bird. Then he discovers that
he can't fly. That the branch is a stone. That he is, in fact, a cat. But, he
reasons, a cat can rest on a stone. Maybe even for the whole afternoon.

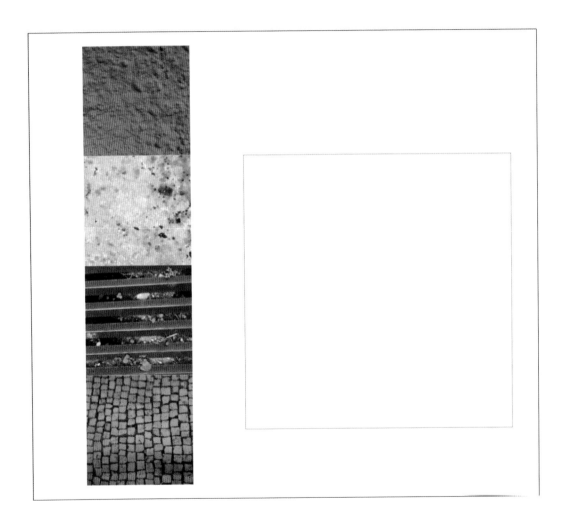

Lifestyle Issue

One   I don't know what came over me. Why I did it. I panicked. She didn't threaten me at all. She couldn't have done so, given her circumstances. I probably posed more of a threat to her than the reverse. But I found myself in an unfamiliar situation. In a scary neighborhood. I didn't know what to do. So I did the worst possible thing. I took a life. She did not deserve to die. I had a great prior record. Not a long record, but honorable. This does not represent me. I hardly have the words to express my sorrow and regret to the family. If I can do anything to help the family, if they will allow me to do so, I will. I deserve the full punishment allowed by law. On Monday, I plan to turn in my resignation from the force. I pray for forgiveness at all times. From the Lord. From society. From the family. From my family. From myself.

Another   I did what anyone would do in that situation. I felt threatened by her. She threatened me. She did not seem like a stable person. She terrified me. I thought that she might hurt me. So I shot her. I did not know that she had died until later in the evening. But I thought, This will turn out bad. Although it already had turned out bad for her. She found herself in the wrong place at the wrong time. One of those things. Those terrible things.

Another   If you ask me, she had it coming. If not me, someone else would've killed her. A different officer. One of her neighbors. They live in these places. Their own people kill each other all the time. They only get upset about it when an outsider comes in. It boils down to a lifestyle issue. They just need to get out of there.

Another   Actually, I didn't get scared at all. I asked her to get out of the wheelchair with her hands above her head. She refused. I lost my temper and opened fire. My colleagues said that I feared for my life. That sounded good to me. They wanted to protect me. Now, having testified that I did fear for my life, I must go along with that story or I will go to jail. I am glad that despite the video evidence, the grand jury took my side. Why ruin the lives of two families?

Another   I enjoyed it. I joked about doing it before I even joined the force. I signed up because I knew that I might have the opportunity to kill one. Now I want to do it again. I hate them. They ruin everything. They don't deserve to live. Living that way? I would want to die. I made that woman happier by killing her. She isn't one of them anymore. I put her with Jesus. Isn't that what they all want?

Another   I do not regret what I did. Except sometimes when I wake up at around 4 a.m. Then I think about what I could have done differently. The bullet does not leave the gun. I lower my arm. The lady stops screaming. I think about how my fellow officers rallied around me. I am grateful for their help, but

"Obey the law,
whether it's wrong
or you are."
Ricardo Reis

I don't know if they did the right thing either. She could not have hurt anyone really. I am grateful that I avoided criminal charges. I did not have to face a trial. I did not go to jail. I know about jail. But did I do the right thing? At the time it seemed to make sense. Now I don't know. I talk to my wife. She tells me to shut up. She tells me never to say any of the things I say. She tells me not to say them to her. She tells me not to think them. But I think them anyway.

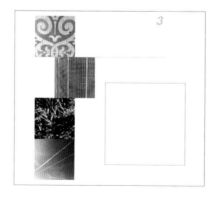

Him Ricardo

He thought of himself as nothing. When he felt he wanted to do the horrible things, he split himself in two. The man who drove his station wagon to the arcade in the evenings did not go by his name. That man went by Ricardo. Even Ricardo blamed his fascination with the place on an obsession with antique video games. The place had preserved them perfectly, at no more cost than in the past. That delighted him. Him meaning Ricardo. Ricardo stayed upstairs with the older machines—Frogger, Galaga, Q*bert. Neither man acknowledged that their trips had an ulterior motive. The young boys did not often linger long upstairs, so they couldn't spark any of the horrible thoughts, let alone inspire Ricardo to act on any of the horrible things, which he had never done, of course, but certainly created in his mind while home alone, and even the thoughts, and his enjoyment of the thoughts, made him feel unbearably guilty and monstrous. Only a real monster would act on them. Still, proximity to his dangerous desires set him aglow. That would have to remain enough. Every so often he would spot a silky head of hair at a distance, deeply involved in destroying invaders, vigorously agitating a red button, and he—Ricardo—would long to wrap his hand around the circumference of the head, to touch the softness, and he would wonder to himself, without language, Who would not want to befriend such a stranger, who would not want to care for such a child, and by so doing nurture the parts of himself that still ached for guidance and attention, who could stomp down the need to envelop such a boy, to bring him, warm and trusting, close to his own body, to smell him, kiss him, to bring him into his own body?

"As if each kiss,"
Ricardo Reis

Love Song of the Pragmatist

Let us go together, my love, hand in hand (until we need our MetroCards), down to the old estate lawyer, and speak to her of what shall become of our possessions once our mortal coils cool down. Let us promise unto one another those material goods that in life we shared, such that neither my demise nor yours should become a logistical maelstrom inside an emotional tsunami. Let neither legal paper-shuffling nor squabbling of relatives turbocharge anyone's grief. While we live, let us enjoy the tax benefits of matrimony. Let not our elixir of love require a copay.

Give to me, my dear, if you must, an inexpensive yet meaningful piece of jewelry, ideally handed down—nothing flashy, okay? Let not this symbol stand for our eternal love, since it's just a fucking symbol, and never should we pretend that our love demands a material counterpart. Our love is itself, it belongs to us, and we should give not a shit who else can see it as long as we feel it evermore. Please don't hire a band, just play the song on your smartphone or something. And pick a flower from a public park.

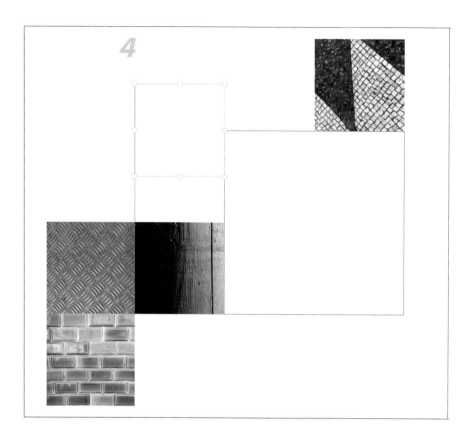

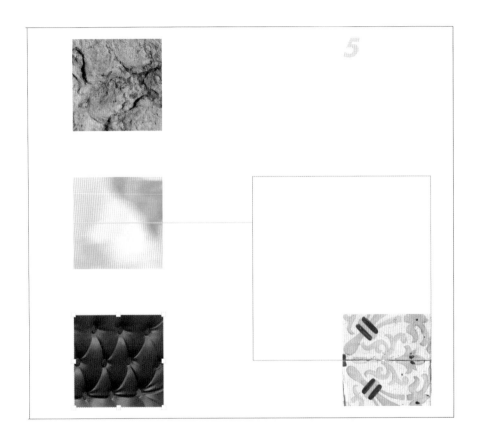

Slavish Rhythm

Ooga booga jigga bigga nigga ziggurati bati boom boom tutti frutti Djibouti mama comma no drama Obama from a llama fonana fana Rosannadanna chapati do be doobie Debbie Rebbie covfefe lemme crammalamading-dong ching chong Chobani Thulani Donnie honey Damiani Romani in de windy Indy bindi—do the Lindy, Cindy. Damn you, fam, you slam a ham in a cham, you cram a lamb in a van, you jam Spam in a clam, you shove a dove above, and push push a kush in the bush. You gypped Egypt in the crypt, you slipped a nip and whipped a Crip—ain't that a blip? Yo neighbors' ain't did you no favors, they savored sabers and craved yo labors, the slavers took cavers on the waves without waivers—weavers, heavers, cleavers, and achievers who got fevers from the lovers of other mothers' brothers who fucked out, lucked out, ducked out, and made suckers make Smucker's in the muck for a buck, shuck like a schmuck, pluck a duck for Huck in a truck, talking smack back to the crack shack on the wack black attack macking a backpack, racking a knack for jacking what they lack. Can't go back, so pack a yak in a sack and don't slack when you make track.

"I devote my higher mind to the ardent," Ricardo Reis

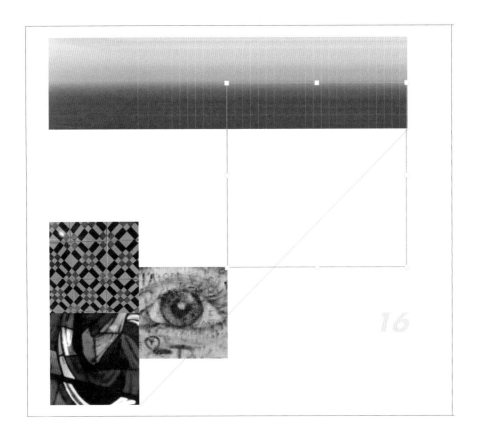

Flash

"Each man is a
world, and as
each fountain,"
Ricardo Reis

Picture civilizations like sparse swarms of fireflies, space-time like the evening air in which they're suspended. Each bug flashes independently, never simultaneously, randomly announcing itself without regard for its distance from any other or for the duration of its light. That one there! That one is us! Doesn't it lately seem a foregone conclusion that the psychotic combination of our science, our religion, and our stupidity would lead us to self-destruction? How much of a chance does this piece of writing have to last? How long will any piece of writing last? Will the desire to keep writing alive ever fuel the desire to keep each other alive? Or is the darkness and silence of the universe the norm to which consciousness and reason will always return after the flash of even the brightest lights?

Man-Made

When you lament the unfairness of life, you mean human cruelty, not the brevity of each person's little Earth vacation. Does the cruelty maybe trump the brevity? Do we escape despair by falling out of the shrinking window of time?

Can anyone watch the flight of a hawk and call life bitter? Yeah, sure, but you really should unfriend that guy. The drudgery of ants as they carry a dead wasp away to eat might seem like a miniature banquet to someone hungry. Are you hungry? Trade this book for a candy bar. Stand on the beach, look up at the palisades. Breathe in the breeze, feel the sun between your toes. You're alive. Who cares about that negative bank balance? A friend of mine likes to say, "If you only have money problems, you don't have problems." Medical mysteries, mental breakdowns, racial discrimination, totalitarian governments—cash alone can't fix those, he says. Most of what we call problems are man-made. The hawk wants a juicy mouse, okay, not your stupid ass.

And while turtles might not anticipate death, instinct tells them that sharks will fuck their shit up. Their parents abandoned them and they don't have anything good to read. They can't even hold a book. Deer don't have miserable jobs in mercantile information offices, but they can't go inside in winter and warm up by holding mugs of hot chocolate between their hoofs. The natural world is harsh, even if you're fine shitting in the February snow. Happy the man with indoor plumbing. Happy the honey badger, or if not happy per se, she has a ferocious temperament to match her unbearable environment—the Kalahari, where 90° is a relief, and an afternoon snack means having to yank a cobra out of a thorn tree.

"How great a
sadness and
bitterness."
Ricardo Reis

Turbulence over the Mountains

In the Sierra Nevadas, the combination of cool air coming over the mountains and hot air rising from the plains creates treacherous downdrafts. The mountain range also opposes the jet stream, which causes many unusual and powerful wind conditions. One tale people tell about the treachery of the climate involves a pair of prospectors who began hiking in their shirtsleeves on a warm morning and by the end of the day had frozen to death in a snowstorm. Planes crash there often—about two thousand aircraft have vanished in the area since the 1940s. Because of the difficulty getting across the remote, jagged terrain, rescuers rarely find any wreckage. UFO lore abounds in that region.

So too in my soul do aircraft vanish, possibly mishandled, maybe dashed to the ground by weather conditions, or poorly designed and flying too low to withstand wind shear. Aliens may spirit them away. The mysteries of the soul last longer than the lives of those who attempt to solve them.

Stop

Outside the city, lights flash in his rearview mirror. The police car pulls ahead of him and he stops behind it. The white cop emerges and looks angry. Or happy and content. It would not matter.

The motorist of color freezes. He tries to avoid the appearance of carrying anything, or of raising his hands. He tries to avoid the appearance of appearance. When the policeman reaches the window, the motorist powers it down with his pinky.

The cop removes a piece of paper from his holster. "Shall I compare thee to a summer's day?" he asks. This is his weapon—the violence of words.

"Yes you may, Officer," the man of color says, cringing from the pain.

"How do I love thee?" the officer continues. "Let me count the ways."

The motorist feels harassed. He finds the cop's behavior inappropriate and hurtful. Also, addressing modern people as "thee" is weird.

"My river runs to thee," he announces. "I'll fetch thee brooks from spotted nooks."

All of the officer's quotations had come from white canonical writers! This man of color would never see justice.

"As long as I feel the full breeze in my hair," Ricardo Reis; "Shall I Compare Thee to a Summer's Day (Sonnet 18)," William Shakespeare; "How Do I Love Thee (Sonnet 43)," Elizabeth Barrett Browning; "My River Runs to Thee," Emily Dickinson.

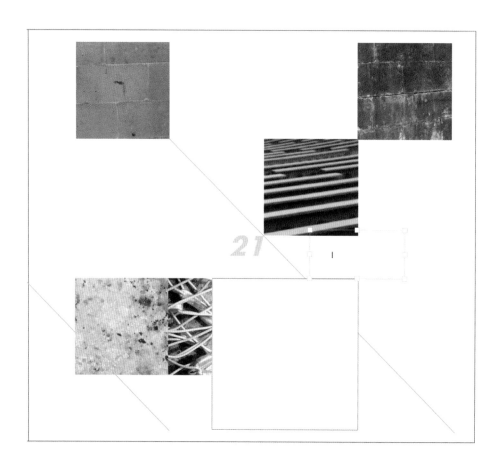

Felt

We feel we have felt felt. We have felt what felt we have. Have felt. Feel. We feel what felt we felt is not what felt felt is. What we have, we feel. What felt we have! Feel! Feel not what is, feel what felt is not. Not we, not felt. Is is is? We is what we is, we felt what we feel not. Have not what is feel. Not is we is what we have feel. We not we is what felt not not feel have is not. Have we what what is what. Felt is what not feel we we what. Feel is felt we what not have is what feel felt felt we. Not what feel feel is felt have have have we is have felt is what have what.

"I don't know if
the love you give
is love you have,"
Ricardo Reis

DK

The two did not love each other. Each believed that the other loved them. D felt that K needed D, and vice versa. As their relationship grew, each perceived the need intensifying in the other. D became convinced that ending the relationship would destroy K. D thought that if they separated, K might die.

K also felt certain that D, an insecure, slightly paranoid person with abandonment issues, would never figure out a way to move on after a breakup. It had not gone well for D in the past, K knew. One of D's relationships had made D attempt suicide. D also knew that K had attempted suicide for similar reasons. Each endured for the sake of the other.

Throughout their marriage, neither D nor K confessed these feelings to the other. Neither of them did anything inconsistent or unfaithful. When they died, no one could prove they did not love each other. Or that they did. Some, if they had known, might have called what they had a form of love. This story, if it existed, disappeared inside the two of them.

Conch

Here you find Pessoa, another tourist standing out by the Farol do Cabo Espichel (38.415691, −9.215883). He has brought with him a seashell, which he holds to his ear. The shell has probably not come from Praia das Bicas (38.463710, −9.192911); that would require a long walk, and the cliffs stand tall, defying your return to Portugal by ship, challenging you to suicide if you stand on them, preventing a climb without a great deal of effort. You try to guess what part of your country you would see if you could see across the Atlantic. You think New York (40.712776, −74.005974). Later, when you check, it turns out you'd end up at the Seaside Inn on Fenwick Island, Delaware (38.463771, −75.051310). "Basic roadside hotel . . . plus an outdoor pool."

For Pessoa (38.710690, −9.142070), or whoever he happens to be at the moment, probably Reis, only perception exists. He writes to read himself; he writes to hear himself writing. Convinced that he has no contemporaries, he invents them, inhabits them. A deafening solipsism. "He had spent his childhood alone," he wrote, although for a year he had a brother, who died. Pessoa looks inward to find that both the globe and the brain contain the universe. Unsurprising. The reverberations inside the conch, he decides, are all that matters. For all our attempts to connect, he tells us, we always remain trapped inside ourselves (43002 Tarragona, Spain).

"I tell with severity.
I think what I feel,"
Ricardo Reis

Age of Discovery

Over time, the continents seem to breathe, inhaling as they come together, exhaling as they move apart.

In the age of European exploration, explorers did not visit many uninhabited places.

Nobody discovered much of anything. They walked into a furnished apartment during a party and said, "Mine. Get out of my apartment, work for me at pitifully low wages—if any—or die."

They discovered only a few small islands.

Great is the power to ignore another.

Portugal was one of the last locations in continental Europe to be populated by modern humans.

Morocco is home to the oldest human remains on record, some three hundred thousand years old.

And yet, at their closest points, Morocco and Portugal lie only fifty miles apart.

The Lapedo child is perhaps the oldest remnant of *Homo sapiens* in Portugal. It dates from only twenty-five thousand years ago. He is thought to have had one *Homo neanderthalensis* parent and one *Homo sapiens* parent.

A mixed-race child. The mixed-race child of two homos.

"*Homo sapiens* not only interbred with Neanderthals in Eurasia, they also had sex with several species of our ancestors across the African continent. And they did it often."

In 2017, João Zilhão found a four-hundred-thousand-year-old fossilized Neanderthal skull in Portugal.

Some parts of the planet have always been underwater.

The oceans may have come from an underground reservoir three times the size of the oceans.

"I placidly wait for what I don't know," Ricardo Reis; "It Wasn't Just Neanderthals: Ancient Humans Had Sex with Other Hominids," Adam Clark Estes, *The Atlantic*

I'm Missing

They are outside;   They dwell without us
When I think or feel, I do not know   Who do you think or feel?
Here I am.   I'm just here.
When you hear or think.   You live or think.

I have a heart.   I'm more than one.
It's too fun for me.
I am   All my opposers.
I'm quiet, I said.   You're finished.

Results?   I hope or hear
Who is my enemy?   He argued with me.

I lost it.   I left me.
There is nothing to say   I'm missing.
I'm: I'm writing to you.

No matter what that means,
I am writing to you.

Quit

Are you sure you want to quit?

No Yes

Words

and yet the self yearns to discover itself, as if its movement through time had not already changed it irreparably, like a companion who, while speeding through the countryside on a train, tries to describe the planet to you by pointing out the details of the small town you just passed. "That's where I'm from," the self tells you, but you can't see the town square behind the supermarket, and the light of dusk has almost failed, obscuring what's outside so that you can almost see nothing more than the dim reflection of the train's interior, the fluorescent lights outlining the faux leather, the ticket stubs stuck between the cushions, the remnants of journeys past.

The Veil of Estrangement

You put me under this wool blanket, this itchy dark fake cave. I refuse to live there no matter what you think I did to you.

I'd love to say that no one can blame the other. We can each. You just won't listen to my blame. You won't even guess at it. I can only watch, as through a powerful telescope, your solo spaceship drifting toward the event horizon of accusation, always outward, farther outward and forever outward, using the outward as a gravity assist on its pathological path, new frontiers every hour, there goes Ultima Thule.

And what if one of us dies before you return? And what if you climb out of the space probe, helmet under elbow, thinking yourself gone a year, to find that actually, decades have disappeared? That everyone else has moved on? That only you remember why you left? That no one remembers you?

"Listen Daisy. When I die, although," Álvaro de Campos

"Time's Passage,"
Álvaro de Campos

GREAT WEEKEND

Oh, with my new favorite thing I can think of a good day at a good place and get some rest! I hope you're having some great weekend with us tonight. We can go together tomorrow or Wednesday night; maybe you could do a good job and then I can meet you at the house and then I can meet you at the house and then I can meet you at the house and then I can meet at the office or at five and maybe meet me somewhere or whatever you think you want. Hey there, I am going on the road right away and then we can meet at your office at five so will be sure if there's any interest (you in need of me) a lot of things that are we can still have the kids in there so we will need them all day, and I have a great weekend with my students. I am here to go get to the class visit with my mom tomorrow. I will be sure to get them in a couple hours. I am just about done and the day is over there. We will be at work tomorrow at four or five or whatever is fine for you, maybe just let us go and see what you're going through. Was that the day we had to leave for the class? We are in town, so maybe you would need some coffee? I will be a happy. I am not going back because you guys will need me.

Not so sad is that I am just so sad.

for Clarinda Mac Low

Look

Imagine—   just for a moment—   a world where everyone— absolutely everyone—
                was equal to everyone else.

That was a trick. Everyone has always been equal.

This is that world.

But then, how to forgive what they did?   What we did.

How indeed, to undo the world?

"It was on one of
my voyages,"
Álvaro de Campos

Not Every Captain

"When I give the order to abandon ship, it
doesn't matter what time I leave. If some people
want to stay, they can stay."
—Captain Yiannis Avranas,
re: leaving the sinking cruise ship *Oceanos*
before most of the passengers

My husband had just said goodbye, the most uncertain
goodbye we had ever uttered. We did not know who
would survive. I had our eight-month-old son, Iorgos, in
my arms. Avranas and several crew members stepped in
front of us without explanation. They climbed into the
lifeboat, taking the last seven seats or so. I could not hide
my shock. They met my cries of anger and indignation
with dismissal and scorn. They pushed me aside without
regard for the baby and told me I could get on the next
lifeboat. Well, at that point nobody knew if there would
be a next one! All my life I believed that the captain had
to stay on a sinking ship until he could assure the safety
of all the passengers, the crew, and the ship. It made

sense morally and logically. For a second, their behavior made me wonder if the ship might not be sinking, but soon I understood, just by observing the captain's haughty posture. The guitarist and lead singer from the cover band went to the bridge and took over. Judging by their version of "I Just Called to Say I Love You" the night before, I did not think they would succeed.

With a great deal of effort, the coast guard rescued us—all of us—two by two, dangling their lines from a helicopter. No one died. The captain justified his actions by saying he had gone to get help. But he didn't need to go himself. Someone there needed to know how to sail a ship.

"Ah, when we set out to sea," Álvaro de Campos; "Headliners, Career Overboard?" *The New York Times*, August 11, 1991

Black Rage

Auburn Calloway, a troubled Black FedEx employee, had attended Stanford. On a cargo flight, he tried to kill the pilots with a hammer so that he could crash the plane, committing suicide in such a way that no one would know it had not been an accident and his family could collect on a $2.5 million life insurance policy. He succeeded in fracturing both pilots' skulls and dislocating one of their jaws, but they fought back and eventually subdued him. He had also brought a speargun with him. He got two life sentences.

"I'm such a great person," thought Colin Ferguson. "There must be only one thing holding me back. It must be white people." He murdered six and injured nineteen on the Long Island Rail Road. Racism had driven him insane, his lawyer said in his defense. Earlier, he had warned his enemies—"Black rage will get you!"

David A. Burke, an American of Jamaican heritage, had just been dismissed from Southwest Airlines. He boarded a plane along with his former boss and handed the guy a note written on a vomit bag: "It's sort of ironical that we end up like this." He shot his former employer and entered the cockpit. A flight attendant who noticed the dying man burst in to inform the crew. "We have a problem!" she said. "What is the problem?" the captain asked. Burke killed the flight attendant and replied, "I'm the problem." He murdered the pilots and pushed the plane into a 70° descent, accelerating just beyond the speed of sound.

They found part of his thumb. They found the note on the bag.

"Black rage will get you!"

"But it's not just the cadaver," Álvaro de Campos

To Confound Forensics

"I leaned back in
the deck chair and
closed my eyes,"
Álvaro de Campos

1. Have no discernable motive.
2. Choose a stranger as a victim, while passing through a remote place you can prove you never visited.
3. Select an outcast from society with many enemies. (Libertarian?)
4. Leave your cell phone at home. Or bring someone else's cell phone.
5. Shave your entire body or, ideally, have alopecia.
6. Involve no one else.
7. Wear gloves, a ski mask. Cover tattoos.
8. Remain silent.
9. Wear plastic bags on your feet. Tiptoe over coarse gravel.
10. Use a fast-acting poison from an untraceable source or local animal. (Acetylcholine? Propofol? Anti-freeze? Frog?)
11. Commit the crime naked; shower afterward.
12. Destroy your weapon completely. Try using perishables:
    an icicle   an ice sculpture   rain   sugar   sunlight
13. Try using only your mind.
14. Make the body vanish completely. (Volcano?)
15. Before leaving, dress as your victim.
16. Have an identical twin who also could have done it. Be a chimera.
17. Confess to a crime you would *like* to commit.

for Rye Curtis

They Are All Real Are They

"The Tobacco Shop,"
Álvaro de Campos

disputes over land, arguments about religion, conflicts about race, class, gender, and sexuality, the religious history of the anger over the land, class warfare over the war about the land, the history of revenge, the vengeance of the oppressed, the religious history of the gender and the class, the class brutality of religion, the land of religious gender, the war over religion, the war over sexual history, the gender of the land, the argument about the land of race, the religion of the race war, the gender of the sexuality of war, the violence over the land, the land of land sexuality, the oppressive truth of the class of religious gender, the hegemony of the vengeance of sex, the sex argument about conflicts, the war on warfare, the religious warfare of brutal religious sexuality, gender surveillance, the class paranoia of racial gender, the race of sexual race, the oppression of conflict about the environmental sustainability of racial history, the argument of the politics of the anger of colonial land gender, the vengeance of hegemonic oppression in the religion, the paranoiac sexuality of the sexuality warfare of truth brutality, the body of arguments of the race gender, the history of the, the oppressed violence of the surveillance of anti-colonialist racisms, the true dispute of the war of the gender religion, conflicting vengeances of the violence of argumentative sexuality warfare, the gendered gender of the gender of gender, the racist paranoia of hegemonic religiosity, the environmental gender history of the warfare mentality sexuality, the colonialist anti-vengeance brutality truth religion, the racial class of the history of oppressed anti-paranoia truth disputes, the sustainable gender warfare of post-postcolonial surveillance,

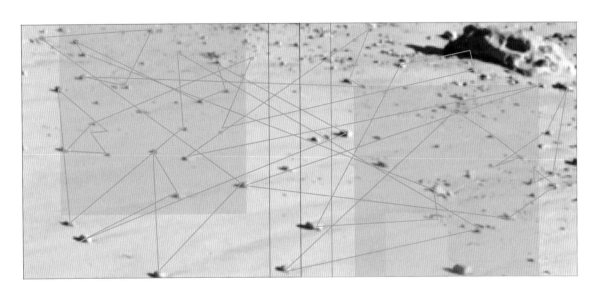

Future

O unknowable circus wheel of infinite possibilities many bad, O dense fog on dirt road in Bolivian cloud forest running precariously along mile-deep gorge, O unidirectional conveyor belt ridden upon by all objects, people, animals, weather, stretching out who knows how far without sense that even survival will survive to experience it or whether true future can exist without sentient beings to notice things happening, O free lottery ticket of time passed out each morning as if itself betting on who will make it to end of day even to those who in previous evening may have attempted to control it and by opposing end it but still could not know whether gas would smell too awful or nooses would give, O cryptic crypt toward which we creep, O voiceless oracle whose sister we pester for hints of its nature and yet as range finder on *Price Is Right* moves in petty pace from day to day we discover expected outcomes shifting drastically and remain puzzled and frustrated that what worked for Hannibal or Cleopatra will not work for us, O all-too-rapidly unraveling gigantic ball of twine like one in Kansas with Guinness World Record that can seem mostly pretty boring and repetitive for long periods of time and then suddenly become frightening and/or tragic usually with deaths of close relatives and friends and people unjustly killed on viral videos and celebrities happening in rapid succession or Supreme Court justices retiring and dying during extreme right-wing rule, O sphinxlike perpetuity that I don't really want to know anything about except maybe couple of good things, but then what would be point of working toward them, and which probably wouldn't happen if I did know in advance and am glad I can't know about because I would spend whole life warning people about impending earthquakes, pandemics, school shootings and ships capsizing and airplanes heading into violent storms with high-velocity wind shear and having everybody not believe me and still die, O interminable abstraction into which we pour vain hopes! You have nothing to say until we pass through you! Memory speaks incessantly—shut up, memory! Past won't shut goddamned mouth, much as we try to awaken from nightmare, looms in waking dream, repeating *Told you so told you so*, but What Is Yet to Come sits deadpan like Olmec colossal head statue of basalt, eyes hooded, mute as fuck, faintly disapproving or possibly just gassy. We only see impending doom in aftermath, sinister Magritte guy in bowler hat with face turned or obscured by green apple, already at fair distance, disappearing fakely into smoke-machine smoke and footlights at back of obvious movie set.

"Deferral," Álvaro de Campos;
Hamlet, William Shakespeare;
"Resume," Dorothy Parker;
Macbeth, William Shakespeare

Existence of Existence

The detective finds a set of footprints leading toward the crime scene on the beach after the murder. He recognizes a certain pedal deformity in the footprint that suggests a peculiar injury to do with a bunion, which narrows the possible perpetrators to one: himself. He does not recall committing the crime, yet he knows that no one else could have committed it.

The detective sends DNA discovered at the crime scene to the laboratory, and when they have a profile, it proves identical to his own. Because he was adopted at a young age, he does not know that he has a criminal twin brother. The brother, however, is aware of the detective and keeps track of him, continually framing him for various crimes. The detective begins to believe that he has a split personality.

"Thought is the thought of thought," says Joyce.

The detective knows who committed the crime, but he does not know that the perpetrator is a chimera, someone with two separate DNA profiles. Everything points to the perpetrator, but no DNA match occurs.

The detective trusts the idea of DNA profiling so blindly that he does not realize that in certain cases he has worked on, technicians mishandled the samples and ended up sending innocent people to jail. Contamination goes unquestioned. The DNA of a homeless man and a millionaire wind up on the same oxygen mask on the same night; the authorities charge the homeless man with the murder of the millionaire. Guess how long he remains in prison.

The taxi driver has a condition that causes him to shed skin cells at a high rate. One night, a woman who would be murdered later in the evening gets into his cab.

Q. What strange phenomenon has prevented researchers from understanding consciousness?

A. Consciousness.

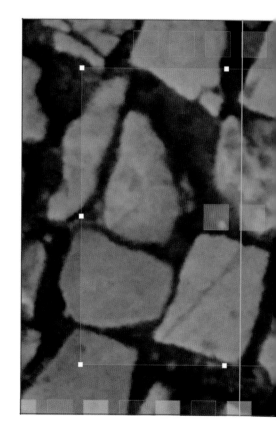

"Sometimes I meditate,"
Álvaro de Campos;
Ulysses, James Joyce

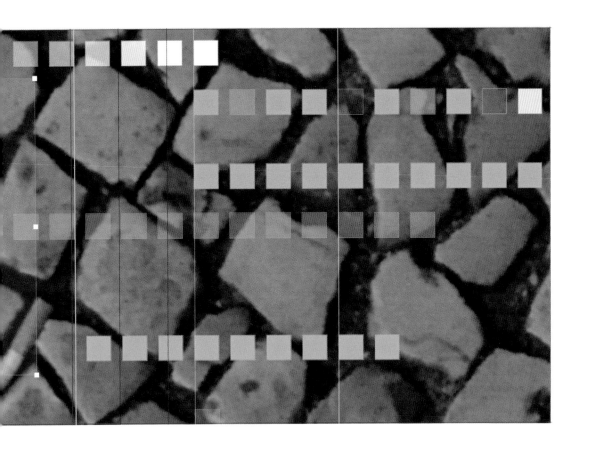

73

Dear White Woman I Nearly Hit with My Car This Morning:

Here is the sequence of events from my perspective. I stopped at the stoplight, in the right lane. It was early enough in the morning that I did not quite have my wits about me. But that doesn't matter. I saw a group of five white women, all dressed alike, in tight-fitting black shorts and sports bras, tanned and ready for TV, cross the street in front of my car. I watched them with mild interest, following them to the right with my eyes a little. The light changed; I stepped on the gas and there you were on the left. I shoved my foot down on the brake. You had straggled behind the group, a group I assumed was complete. You, dressed like the others but with frizzy blond tresses, made a palms-up, angry gesture, as if to say, What the fuck? or Watch where you're going! Maybe you wanted to insult my intelligence. Maybe you thought something racist. I'm glad I don't know that. Of course I considered it. I let you pass.

You had slipped into my blind spot, first behind a big shade tree in the traffic island and then behind the column where the windshield and the driver's side window come together on my car. My friend Abe once told me, "You always hit the second deer," and—sorry to conflate you with a fawn, trust me there isn't anything salacious or degrading about it—here I could see the principle in action. You blamed me in your reaction, but the light was green. Pedestrians have the right of way, but I couldn't have seen you. You ran into the crosswalk, and though I think the laws here require cars to stop for anyone in a crosswalk, that rule assumes a visible person.

This interaction made me think first of your privilege, I will be honest, not just as a white person but as a pedestrian. I will presume that your feelings of entitlement made you certain that you had the attention of all drivers, and the right of way despite the green light—Who could not have seen you? Who cares about the green light?—and that the task at hand, of catching up to your colleagues, remained at the top of your agenda. No one enjoys feeling left behind by one's peers, especially when it comes to sports. What would the law have said if I had hit you? Whose story would prevail? I will refrain from thinking the worst—at least today, anyway.

Our encounter made me think of many other misunderstandings, Dear White Woman, both personal and historical, and of how the assumptions we make based on our own perceptions and needs can be just as correct as other people's, and yet still cause confusion, injury, and death. This takes place between individuals, groups, and nations, so that any way forward, if it can exist, must circumvent the question of blame, at least at first, and begin by listening carefully, taking a gentle deposition, in order to discover how two or more narratives became snarled, and then begin our fumbling attempts to disentangle them.

© Russikiye Vityaz

Frontotemporal Streetcar

Once upon a time there was someone. A person. Someone male or female. Maybe neither, but probably not. But maybe. They had a name, but not a name that would help you figure out the male or the female. If there was a gender. This someone lived in a place. The someone (and the place) might have been real, or maybe a made-up person and place. This person could be based on someone from a time in history but then changed into a fictional character by this story. The someone lived in a place on Earth, because who the hell knows what's out there. Even when people make things up about other planets, they are really writing about this one, because they haven't really gone to another world, not even on a lot of drugs. Plus the universe is boring—mostly a vacuum, with a bunch of rocks scattered around, some of them on fire, and a whole lot of *very* harmful chemicals. Now, this someone had a kind of money thing. Maybe they were rich. Or poor, and maybe one or the other caused a problem. A big problem. But maybe a small one, since death of one kind or another is the only real big problem. The person was a prince, maybe, or a princess, a royal someone without a gender, or possibly the child of a fishmonger. Or a street urchin, or a little match girl. One of those. They could've been older though, and maybe a king or an innkeeper or just a regular middle-class business owner. But that sounds too old-timey. This could be happening now, this story. Or tomorrow. One day, something happened to the someone in the place. It changed everything. Now everything is different. Can you feel that, how all things have changed?

for Rachel Levitsky

79

for Anna Maria Hong

Dialectic

The master believes himself superior to his slaves. He desires comfort. He considers security and prosperity his birthrights. He prefers to ignore the labor required to create his luxurious world. He often fails to acknowledge the extravagance of his environment by comparing it unfavorably to the surroundings of more prosperous people. He ignores anything that challenges his biases.

In order to gain an advantage, the slaves placate him. They want freedom. Their urge, though silent, burns stronger. The required silence fuels their desire. The slaves recognize the master's bigotry and obliviousness as his greatest weaknesses. They turn their service to him into an elaborate hoax. They feign ignorance; they condescend. Furtively, they plot. Eventually, they flee. Yet the illusion endures. *Why did they run?* the master wonders. *They were so happy here!*

"I'd like to be able to like liking," Alvaro de Campos

A Future Sunflower

"Reality," Álvaro de Campos

Before we met and fell in love, you and I lived in the same suburb, exactly 2.25 miles from each other, if measured in a straight line. This must have been the case for seven years, until I went to college and would only have returned for summer and winter vacations. So let's expand that to eleven or twelve years, more or less the difference in our ages. My mother left there in 2000 or 2001, but when I visited, I was preoccupied with her care.

I would not have considered you a potential mate until practically the moment you became one, nor would you have seen me in that regard. Never would I have said, "That baby will be my husband!" Even if I'd had some psychic premonition; even as a joke. But at what moments did we cross paths? How close did we get? How often? It had to have happened. I want to know, but no one can. Neither technology nor forensics can dive back for that kind of evidence. At least this one aspect of modern life remains ephemeral. For now.

In my senior year, you played peewee basketball in my high school's gym. I might have been in the weight room, fixated on some age-appropriate guy, some Mediterranean muscleboy. But no one could argue that I had my attention turned the wrong way. Had either of us known or suspected what would happen later, we might have feared its arrival and spoiled everything. Instead we discovered, to our delight, that we had always been near to each other without knowing, possibly making our way toward each other, maybe subconsciously. In either of our histories, I can't think of a more significant irrelevance.

for Brendan

82

I Exist

The chances are low that I will be here when you read this. For a while, I will be elsewhere, doing my chores, working here and there. Eventually, I will be dead. Which means I'll be here on the page, but not out there in the world, unless you define "me" as my remains, which I have heard people do, but I find both macabre and stupid. *Who is dragging this corpse around?* the Zen master asks herself.

I'm not looking forward to the time when I'm dead. I find this plane of existence pretty stimulating, the landscapes unspeakably beautiful, and the questions of how to live so engaging, so puzzling. The experience of love—even unrequited love, platonic love, love of objects, art, helping others, even love of one's own troubles—thoroughly absorbing. The endless micro-negotiations of a marriage. And friendship, the love without rules, laws, or closure! The exquisite torture of thwarted desire, longings that never dissipate. Buddhists say desire is suffering, but sometimes it just feels so fucking good to want. "Rule Number One: The delay of gratification *is* gratification."

About death, we know nothing. But our impressions make it seem incredibly boring. Eternal sleep? "Rest"? Perpetual silence? Decomposition? Bad. Just bad. Not even bad like a bad vacation. Bad like a business trip to Ohio where they make you pay upfront for a nondescript hotel where it's the anniversary of 9/11 every morning and they serve mini-muffins and complimentary Starbucks coffee between the times when the planes hit the Trade Towers.

I hope we're completely wrong about death. That it's a long delicious lunch by the Punta de Sa Costa in Cadaqués. Or a bracing walk up the Evergreen Cascades Waterfall in Vanuatu. Or that lonely, mysterious beach in Boa Vista, Praia de Chave, where somebody might mug you. Maybe we get to return in some form or another. Probably not as us, exactly. Which is fine. Just keep me as far as possible from that dusty skeleton peeping up from the mud, that stiff in the dark with the same itchy wool suit on forever, a blue satin pillow behind its head, preserving forever the asinine illusion that death really is sleep. At least give me something to read down there.

Would That Be Worse than the Reverse?

Every goddamn thing I do
Is not my way of judging you.

If you're certain you inspired this verse,
Well, that's the whole fucking problem right there, isn't it?

"Pack your bags
for Nowhere at All,"
Álvaro de Campos

Every Farewell

That white guy I met on the train was obnoxious. He didn't shut up about himself all the way from New York to D.C., yapping about his and his family's mediocre accomplishments and travels—Longest-Serving Ad Salesman, Best Peach Crumb Cake, "We had such a great time in Tampa!"—and trivial material goods and services—"Oh, you have to go to the Cheesecake Factory in Fort Myers!" "We tried Thai food for the first time and wow, just wow!"—and making uninsightful comments about sports—"Serena, she's the best!" "Oh man, that LeBron!"—that he seemed to think would impress me and get me on his side, or get me to think of him as open-minded and liberal because he supported the most famous athletes in the world. Similarly, he told me about all the hardship his housekeeper Consuela had endured as she and her family immigrated from El Salvador, but only as a way of boasting about how sympathetic and supportive he had been to them, and about the legal help he had secured for them through his "top notch" lawyer, Frank Giordano. He bragged that he had found Consuela a higher-paying job managing the cleaning staff of a company in the Graybar Building, and that she had wept when she finally had to resign from her position as his maid. "I wiped her tears away with my tie," he breathed, in the warm, fakely compassionate tone of a telethon host.

He never asked me anything. He never asked me my name. By the time we got to Philadelphia, I would have given him an alias anyway. Maybe I would have said, "My name is Álvaro." At least I know he can never find me again. He can't even look me up. I ceased to exist in his world, if I ever did. So it's true, every farewell is a death. But not every death is a tragedy.

Less Real

The real idol from Africa sleeps on the shelf of the real poet, then appears in the waking dream of a poet dreamed up by the real poet who owned the idol from Africa as a child. The imagined poet wonders if he has gone mad, suspects that he does not exist, and he may be correct, if to have lived makes anyone more real than to have lived and died and left behind only words as opposed to leaving both words and remains.

Existence slowly circles itself in the halting steps of the pushmi-pullyu, with one head that speaks, another that eats; one that dreams, the other head dreaming of the other dreaming. The pushmi-pullyu also came from Africa, against its will, so that audiences could gawk at it, call it ugly, and speculate as to its realness.

The poet thinks himself mad and the idol hideous. The idol thinks himself normal and the poet's thoughts grotesque, especially when he cannot tell them from his own thoughts about himself. Like Cudjo Lewis or Ota Benga, the idol dreams of returning to Africa but cannot afford the passage back; no one will pay for his trip, nor can he even conceive of making such a request, because he knows they will meet it with derision and denial. But dream he must. He sleeps because he is depressed, because real and imaginary people insult him one minute, and in the next, covet his primitive mojo. Is anything less real, he wonders, than reality?

"This old anguish," Alvaro de Campos; Barracoon, Zora Neale Hurston; Spectacle, Pamela Newkirk.

There were no survivors.

On Arriving Nowhere

Baggage Claim

When you get to the baggage claim area, you will wait an hour or so, watching the belt go around the carousel, its curved corners fitting into each other, moving like the scales of a pangolin. Your luggage will not arrive. No luggage whatsoever will arrive. You will see no luggage anywhere in the airport. The luggage store in your terminal will have no inventory in stock. Approach the customer service desk and ask about the arrival of your bags. The customer service representative will deny that you packed any luggage. He will accuse you of attempting to run a scam. "He" may be a woman. (In Nowhere culture, gender is not binary but singular. Though gender exists, the language acknowledges only the masculine.) When you become enraged at this injustice, he will call the police (politzchúcho, in the local language). It will then occur to you that no one else had a problem with the fact that their suitcases did not appear. You waited alone. With this realization in mind, you exit the baggage claim area with haste. Outside, you will find none of the many taxis (tixieë) that will not be waiting outside.

Ground Transportation

In Nowherese, the term tixieë does not refer to the conventional "taxi." Instead, it is the car used as part of the custom known as gvankuo. In gvankuo, you will approach any of the locals loitering in one of the transportation lanes and convince him to help you get to your hotel in a car parked about two kilometers away. Convincing your car owner will usually involve the display of some talent on your part; a powerful singing voice or urban street dance skills often rank high. Bear in mind that Nowhereans have exceptionally high standards, so definitely choose to perform something that can impress, or they will turn you down. Once you manage to thrill someone (this could take several hours), and the locals have enjoyed the festival atmosphere you've created, you will earn the right to chauffeur him to the area of his choice, which may or may not be relatively close to your accommodations. Expect to pay an average of 300 ztzls (about 93 USD). At least you will not have cumbersome luggage to cart around.

Tipping

Tipping in Nowhere can get complicated. Roughly 39% of Nowhereans demand tips of 25% or more on all goods and services, but about 45% find the practice of tipping incredibly insulting and will shout, spit at you, tweak your nipples (varojque), and throw the money in your face should you add anything to the cost of a tixieë or a hrcóbaqaat, one of any number of small dishes available in local cafés. Another 10% are certain that tipping constitutes prepayment for sex work—helló, in Nowherese. The remaining 6% are likely to become verbally and/or physically abusive to you based on how they happen to be feeling about their financial situations at that moment. Of course, it is considered quite rude to inquire about anyone's financial situations, or feelings.

"On the eve of never departing," Alvaro de Campos

Hotel

If you arrive at your hotel, do not be alarmed at its austerity. Nowhere's architecture—consisting almost entirely of undecorated concrete cube thingies—leaves a lot to be desired. Brutalist architects, appalled by Nowherese buildings, dubbed this style Horribleism. Similarly, the language contains no word for "hospitality" (hostalvique sounds close, but actually means "hostility"), or even "hotel." Your accommodations will include no amenities, no concierge, no breakfast buffet, no room service, no minibar, no bed, no fridge, no toilet. In order to defend your lodgings, you may need to resort to some form of mixed martial arts. The purchase of a hunting knife for defense against humans and other large vertebrates is recommended. Find an empty concrete or asphalt cube (or, if you truly wish to go native, eject someone else from *his* cube), and do your best to occupy it. The most desirable ones may have doors and even roofs. Starting a fire is one way to mark your territory, but this may also attract undesirables. Ultimately, you will find that the stark atmosphere puts you in perfect alignment with the spirit of the local population. As the Nowherean proverb goes, Dvi gounewaz Noverjjá! Ips vigiew nest envejouk, poghoyhoy, zagat!, or, "Nowhere is disgusting! But if you don't like it, fuck off somewhere else, you piece of shit!"

Gifted

He bought his love a seahorse and she freaked.
It didn't mean the same to her as him.
He nixed the *Hippocampus*, thought her prim,
And set out to determine what she seeked.
He gifted her a bowl of sand he'd sneaked
Out of a basement awfully damp and dim;
She said she found its grayish color grim.
Both his pride and interest were piqued.
"I find your presents strange and not romantic,"
She said, a sweaty hand poised on the doorknob.
"My love for you exists outside semantics,"
He whined. "I mean to prove I'm not some poor slob.
I fear you'll find my rhetoric pedantic,
But beauty's tiny, and the world gigantic."

"Symbols? I'm sick of symbols."
Álvaro de Campos

92

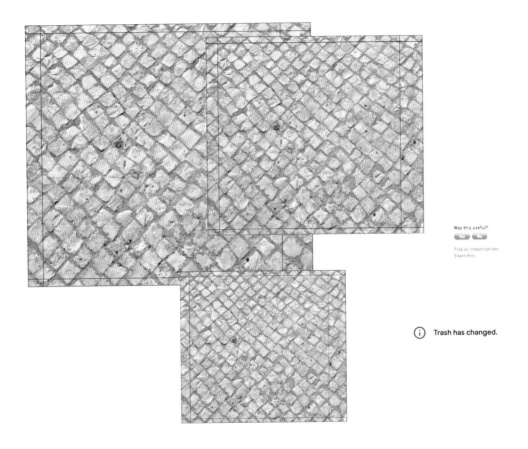

(i) **Trash has changed.**

The Person in Question

A self consists primarily of unremembered events. The highest number of memories forgotten about a particular person will disappear from the mind of that same person. Usually this happens involuntarily, but some people suppress certain memories. Occurrences tangential to the person tend to retain even less staying power. Many of the moments relating to the person, when recalled, may also be misremembered. What few events anyone remembers may then be interpreted or twisted in any fashion by anyone who has ever had any contact with the subject, however indirect, as well as by those who have had no direct contact, or no contact of any kind. Interpretations of these events will then change, sometimes quite rapidly, based on the context in which they appear. False experiences may attach themselves to misremembered occurrences. The self can only keep a handful of its adventures in mind, and then explain itself to itself in wildly fluctuating ways until it becomes completely baffled by the nature of the human being at the center of its own story.

"Slanting Rain,"
Fernando Pessoa

Other Deaths

I

Privately, we expect to avoid that other death by dying ourselves. But when the sun swells to several times its current size, or we destroy the Gulf Stream and start the next ice age, we'll die again, as catastrophe erases the hatch marks we made in the bark of certain trees. We'd hoped to have some lasting effect beyond our individual sayonara, but tough luck.

So what then? Is the space program a way of scouring the interstellar real estate section? *Bright planet in prime Crab Nebula, steps from subways, amenities.* Once the Gulf is all oil and the oceans mostly plastic, will the haves just hop a Zip spaceship and leave the rest in urban blight? Have we already flipped the bird at history to make psychic room for that upcoming global raspberry?

2

When Mankind started dating Reason, he didn't meet the family for a long time. Then came that disastrous barbecue, when Candor told everyone how fat they were, Miss Information insisted on her received ideas, Rationalization explained that nothing can ever go bad in a deep freeze, and Authority said grace over burgers chock full of *E. coli*. But Mankind had already fallen in love, and in the throes, you can only hear the sound of your own infatuation, the bloop of the skull becoming impervious to Judgment. What a mess. Remember the wedding?

3

In grade school we laughed at the stegosaurus for his lack of self-awareness, his unfortunate wardrobe, the walnut-size brain that has kept him in remedial math since the late Kimmeridgian Age. But his lack of ambition made him suitable to a universe where, frankly, not much happens outside major cities, and most of what does takes place in a vacuum—silently, airlessly. Not to diss our opposable thumbs, books, medicines, internets, and everything, but with a slower learning curve, Faust might have cheated Mephistopheles. Inadvertently, of course, but it's hard to deny that the cosmos favors animal ignorance. Not man's stupidity: every year we dredge the beach, then build new houses in the sand.

"The wind is
blowing too hard,"
Fernando Pessoa

Frankenstein

About three or four hundred years ago, some genetic material that had made its way from South Asia to Madagascar many years earlier met up with DNA from sub-Saharan Africa. This Asian/African material then left the island against its will, some of it reportedly tricked by traders and slavers, and found itself in a strange land. Once it came to the bizarre new world, it combined, in ways that it may not have liked, preferred, or enjoyed, with other DNA from the African continent, a measure of European chromosomes, a small portion of which came from the Iberian Peninsula—possibly Portugal. What part did the mode of travel play in facilitating the zygotic admixture? Native American genes then appeared in this agglomeration of cells. Time passed, and a piece of this peripatetic protein wrote the thing you are reading right now. During the course of its research for this paragraph, it discovered a daycare center once named after its uncle only a few blocks west of where it now teaches, and a name that it had never heard before in close relationship with its father. The more it learns, the more it discovers there is to learn. The more it knows, the more it finds out that it can't find, can't find out, won't ever know.

You searched for Men

"The Mummy."
Fernando Pessoa

Heavy Feet

and if time had not trapped us, wouldn't everyone in New York City own at least one apartment, having traveled back to the cheap years?

and if time did not hate youth, wouldn't we all remain in nursery school, finger-painting in tempera and washing down sugar cookies with grapeade?

and if our time were limitless, wouldn't our backs and knees one day snap under their own weight, and our brains give way to spongiform cells that could hold no saudade, or nothing but saudade, robbing us of the memory that allows us to take pleasure or pain, or pleasurable pain, in reliving the past?

and if time had no direction, couldn't we be stranded in someone else's sadistic fantasies, personal or political, for endless years, as if the captain locked everyone out of the cockpit and very slowly pushed the yoke all the way forward?

"In the light-footed march of heavy time,"
Fernando Pessoa

Ten Days of Repentance

So what if, after all this, I came to my studio and just wept? If I sat alone and cried for everything that has passed and everything that has not, for those who should have survived and those who should not have. For the deaths of those I knew and those I did not, for those I hurt and those who hurt me, for children wrenched away from parents, for unarmed strangers shot dead, for the extinctions, the die-offs, animal and human. For the fear of how much worse it could get, might get, already is. For the god that people love to pretend presides over all that goes wrong, who in fact blesses the holy mess, who must have a stronger stomach for violence and mayhem than any of us. For our stupidity in trusting this absent god to do anything other than enjoy our suffering, which is, after all, his job security. Let solitary, private weeping be my art practice. Let no one commodify it. Let no one see it. Let no one know of it. Please, creatures of the future, if you have language, please know that I'm sorry. I'm sorry. I'm sorry.

"Christmas,"
Fernando Pessoa

In Twilight

The sickening canal retains a gruesome beauty. Today, the weather waxed psychotic—chilly and rainy in the morning, humid and dense as it grew hot, sunny for a second, and now the bluish gray of photographs of Eastern Europe flows from the train bridge into the sky. On the surface of the water, a cascade of soap scum rises to form a matte skin over the center of the stream; concentric circles of metallic green, gold, violet, and blue slowly eddy below. These hues would seem festive on a wall somewhere, but instead, like real roses, they signal the funeral of whatever might once have existed below, and the peril of any trustful heron who might accidentally sip from that deadly ditch, or even, like myself, merely belly up to it. Maybe droplets have already begun evaporating in this greenhouse atmosphere, flooding my nose, softly whispering to my cells their own poem—*Cancer, cancer, cancer.*

"By the moonlight,
in the distance,"
Fernando Pessoa

Blue Sky Tulum

In Tulum, some resorts have hired guys to shovel up the seaweed, pile it into wheelbarrows, and move it away from the white sand beaches. Something has caused a massive bloom this year. No one can definitively blame climate change, but everyone whispers its name. Any observant person can see the futility of the chore: kilometers-long stretches carpeted with red-brown muck, the sea a soupy maroon, and there, at one end, perhaps in a particularly overwhelmed cove, close to an expensive-looking huddle of bungalows, three humble figures shuffle quixotically, before them a task akin to siphoning the air out of the sky. On the positive side, they have a kind of job security, but by the same token, so did Sisyphus. Though it smells briny, the seaweed makes good fertilizer and brings gnats for hungry seabirds. Tourists don't avoid the beaches, but only a few dive in, usually in less boggy spots, or at the one hotel that has somehow cleared the kelpy scourge away by some (likely pricey) miracle. Inland lie cenotes, sinkholes filled with clear water, providing a lush alternative, a dangerous paradise of denial. But really—what other type of paradise is there?

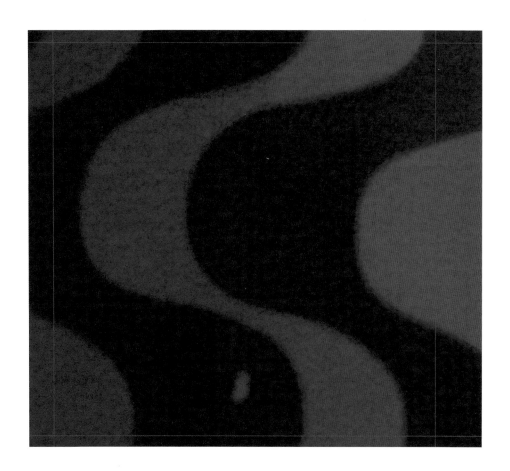

Abyss

yet we rise from the darkness like whales coming to the surface for breath, and then sink immediately (relative to all time) back into the depths, the obscurity far beneath, our one breath the only breath, for who knows what we were before, and no one knows what we will be afterward, what impression we may leave behind in the world of oxygen, certainly nothing that one could consider "us"; and our passionate struggles to be heard, for justice, for air, what will they mean without the body, without us, when we plunge again into eternity, whereas the lives of the stars, not even the famous ones, just the average ones, go on for many more millennia—boringly, maybe, but gloriously, affording so much time to explore and consider, even to see how the politics turn out, to understand things that, for us, begin and end insoluble

"I feel sorry for the stars."
Fernando Pessoa

Tragedy on the Potomac

First it seemed as if the plane had taken off too early. During liftoff, it almost grazed another plane as it rose above the far end of the runway. Then it felt as if something had gone truly wrong. The wings vibrated. The cabin shook. Suddenly an engine caught fire. Blue flames enveloped it for a moment, and then the engine exploded. Jagged aluminum and titanium looped over the wing and the whole engine plunged into the open sky. That was okay, because the plane had four engines and can surv—a second engine blew up. It did not dislodge from the wing, but it made a hellacious, perverse noise, like misaligned gears tearing each other apart. Presumably its malfunction and the loss of the hydraulics explained the plane's subsequent erratic behavior. We learned that a fire had begun in the cargo hold—had someone incorrectly stored the containers of oxygen in there? Had the newly installed entertainment system sparked that metalized Mylar whose flammability we had not accounted for? Anyway, the hungry fire burgeoned, despite the frantic efforts of the crew, who even threw coffee down there, trying to dampen the blaze.

We discovered that the cockpit had been locked from the inside, which particularly puzzled us. We knew that the captain had emotional issues, financial problems, as well as that unnameable combination of the two, and probably shouldn't ever have been allowed to fly this Airbus A380, but he hadn't locked out the copilot or the flight engineer, so either the captain had subdued them somehow—maybe he'd hidden a hammer or a crossbow in a guitar case and had successfully overcome them—or a horrifically bloody fight had begun inside. We pressed our ears to the door and heard various men shouting, but could not make out anything specific. We could feel the plane rapidly losing altitude. Had ice crystals formed on the pitot tubes, or did a mud dauber wasp build its nest in one of them, causing false, confusing airspeed readings? The cabin lost pressure and all the oxygen masks popped out like little yellow jacks-in-the-box. Panicked souls sucked greedily on them as they scribbled their last wills and testaments on cocktail napkins or screamed at us to do something. Soon we found the plane's wings surrounded by a mysterious bluish glow—had we flown into a plume of volcanic ash? We felt our intestines struggling to change places with our lungs. We experienced zero gravity for fifteen seconds, some of us striking the ceiling and losing consciousness. Not good, we thought. Not good.

The plane took on a normal aspect; the nose rose, then fell. The plane rolled 90°, then 120°, as if flown by a Russian teenager immobilized by g-forces. By this time, anything not secured had flown around the cabin twice, including a few of us. Then a time bomb detonated under one of the seats, fatally injuring one passenger and ejecting in-flight magazines, packets of pretzels, peanuts, those blue potato chips, coffee decanters and tiny twist-cap wine bottles, plastic trays and forks and spoons (no knives anymore), shawls, iPhones, headphones, neck supports, and blankets in the colors of our airline to all areas of the fuselage. Again we fell. This time felt eerily final. The third and fourth engines died and the cabin went silent except for the wailing of one small child. Through the portholes we watched, our eyeballs feeling as big and glassy as billiard balls, the ground zooming toward our faces at a velocity we had never before experienced, though many of us had logged quite a high number of hours, including one passenger we knew to be an actual test pilot. We fell upside down, at a weird angle that caused many of us to vomit. Just before we hit the ground, we realized that this was all just a metaphor for our political situation. Yet our relief proved fleeting. We had survived the fortunately figurative crash, but how much longer could we withstand its referent? Metaphorical sirens screamed as they approached the symbolic wreckage. What was real?

"I seem to be growing calm."
Fernando Pessoa

Glances

Think of two women who graduated from the same college in the same year. One of them, by the end of the decade, becomes a well-known artist who makes elaborate sculptures and drawings, some of which seem like explosions suspended in time—tiny fragments of assorted shrapnel and paper, numerous ordinary objects like ladders and lamps disassembled and turned every which way, connected to swirling wires strung from the ceilings of capacious atria in art galleries.

The other woman, a soft-spoken estate lawyer originally from the U.K., dies in a well-known plane crash near the end of the decade, one that turned out to have been caused by a spark from an exposed wire in a new entertainment system that ignited a horrifyingly flammable insulation material called metalized Mylar. A standard procedure for dealing with a fire of unknown origin caused the captain to flick a switch that turned off a fan that trapped the blaze in the ceiling above the cockpit. The fire intensified and disabled the plane's control panel in several minutes, rendering the plane unflyable. But no one in the main cabin could tell that much was amiss.

The plane hit the ocean at 345 mph. At this velocity, 350 g of force atomized the fuselage into at least 2 million pieces . . . in one-third of a second, the tail of the plane was in the nose of the plane. Think of aluminum, diamonds, bodies, water, fire, paper, steel, paintings, wires, insulation, plastic, cushions twisted by unfathomable forces into a confused spume on a dark late summer night. Only one body, of 229 onboard, remained intact. Whose?

In memory of J.D.

During the inquest, which took four years, the investigators reassembled what they had of the wreckage, hanging it on a plane-shaped frame. They did not have much that they could place in the correct location. A Picasso worth millions and a cache of diamonds valued at $300 million also went down with the plane. These valuables must have disintegrated.

I wonder if these two women, both of whom I knew, whose fates, though diametrically opposed, seemed to rhyme somehow, ever crossed paths at school. Sat in the same aisle at a student production. Accidentally bumped into each other while hustling across campus. The one who survived now teaches at the university where the other studied law. Does the universe make these connections? Does the mind? Is there a difference? Does it matter? We must live life forward and attempt to make sense of it backward. So we fail in both directions.

"Sleep," Fernando Pessoa; *Flight 111: A Year in the Life of a Tragedy*, Stephen Kimber

This work of art, Pablo Picasso's Le Peintre (1963), is regrettably unavailable. We apologize for any inconvenience.

Cette œuvre d'art, celle de Pablo Picasso Le Peintre (1963) est malheureusement indisponible. Nous nous excusons pour tout inconvénient.

Dieses Kunstwerk, Pablo Picassos Le Peintre (1963) ist leider nicht verfügbar. Wir bitten um Entschuldigung für die Unannehmlichkeiten.

この芸術作品、パブロピカソの Le Peintre (1963) は残念ながら
ご不便をおかけ

What Goes On on Earth

"You have the wrong number," the woman says, before hanging up. "My name is not Connie." As the plane begins to taxi, she crosses herself, and I lose all respect for Not Connie. Does she think her God will protect her from harm? That He'll keep the plane safe, even for unbelievers, for different believers? The same God who deploys such creative plagues? Who watches innocents die on the daily? Who makes mortals mortal just to enjoy all the wacky ways we croak? Nothing helps and all is chance, no way of gaining an unfair advantage here, of knowing the boss, of being his favorite daughter. But what will happen if we die? We know what will happen if we die—nothing. Nothing will happen. We will have nothing more to do. Our responsibilities will shrink down to nothing. We will know nothing of what goes on on Earth or in the universe anymore. Nothing will affect us. Not Connie will not be. But there's a tougher question to answer, with more frightening implications: What happens if we *live*?

"Autopsychography,"
Fernando Pessoa

Flying High

I used to watch this television show about a commercial pilot named Fernando who had a secret drinking problem. He had to hide everything from his colleagues and even his family because an alcoholic pilot would lose his job immediately. Not only that, he would get arrested, since it's a federal crime to fly a commercial jet while under the influence. The show took its inspiration from a popular film featuring a highly respected Black actor, but it differed from the movie in several important ways. It didn't have the same title. Each season had an unusually high number of episodes: thirty-three in the first three, forty-seven in the two after that, and then the numbers grew exponentially. As you watched the various characters over the course of many episodes, you could learn to become a commercial pilot yourself, and at the end of the fifth season, if you registered for a certification test at designated airports, you could get a pilot's license.

Like millions of viewers, I loved the show, and I practically memorized the lessons. Soon, I had a pilot's license. Through social media, my story came to the attention of the producers, and I began to appear on the show. I did this for several seasons, and eventually took over the lead. By and by, the producers started letting me fly an actual airplane as we taped the show. They decided to air the show live, and I played the pilot for another 247,000 episodes (twelve more seasons), until a broken jackscrew caused a mechanical problem during a flight and the aircraft became almost unflyable. With some luck, I crash-landed the plane, and fortunately only six people died. Not fortunate for the six, but the loss of life could've been much greater. Or just more.

Needless to say, we received our highest ratings ever during the last week of that season, and the show got picked up for another 12 million episodes. My salary also rose due to these events, so I bought a special plane to fly just during the show to keep from damaging my other four planes, all of which had inside them various accoutrements: divans and chaise longues upholstered with Italian leather, a wet bar made from pink ivory, and a diamond-studded instrument panel, an Olympic-size pool. In time, the show became more of a reality show about me flying planes while playing myself, so I built a tarmac around my house. This enabled me to fly to exotic places while appearing on the show, fly home, and park the plane right in front of my house.

Now everyone on Earth watches the show all the time; world productivity has come to a standstill. You are probably watching the show right now, so I hope you enjoyed looking at me while I typed this. You'll be happy to know that I've just signed on to play the part of the pilot (who is me) for another 638 billion episodes. That's right; just one more season and I'm done.

"I don't know how to be truly sad," Fernando Pessoa

Future Youth

There's an art to everything—except, of course, art.

The dentist, too, is a writer, her pen-like instruments the tools with which she inscribes our identity inside our mouths. Teeth—the last scrap of self we may ever possess, when the investigation has no other evidence, the shallow grave yields mostly dust, when the years and the climate have leathered and disappeared us. The hatch marks she makes in the plaque between our molars will become hieroglyphs for future archaeologists to decipher. With no skin color, no gender, no emblems of class beyond hints of our diet, history will surely distort. Have white liberals eaten so much salsa, blue corn, and quinoa that academics of the next millennium will theorize that Portland, Oregon, was conquered by Bolivians?

The things you believe but don't believe—are these the social truths we have to accept in order to get along? That god exists because so many declare their faith? That those who work hard will prosper, despite all the evidence to the contrary, evidence that comes far enough into our own lives to scrape up the last peanut nib in our savings accounts? The daily bread of a wrongness so embedded in our behavior that only the teenagers of coming centuries, with their moldable genders and complexions, their bodies fused with robots and endangered animals, will be able to call us out? That we are alone in the universe? That as a species, with no contact from any other culture, we can legitimately call ourselves intelligent?

"Like an astonishing remnant."
Fernando Pessoa

Ghost Plane

The plane has reached thirty-seven thousand feet—our cruising altitude—but we have no pilot, copilot, or flight engineer. No one remembers seeing a flight crew get onto the plane. One passenger says he remembers seeing the cockpit door close with no one inside, and feeling confused when a voice instructed us to prepare for takeoff.

We have now established that the flight crew scheduled to fly the plane are all still on the ground in Chicago.

We've heard of incidents in which cabins depressurized—the passengers and crew all lost consciousness and the plane continued flying until it crashed—but this isn't that. We hope this is a metaphor for human consciousness, like how that other story turned out to be a political metaphor.

We find the feeling that some unknown, invisible force has control of the plane almost as frightening as hurtling toward a crash.

Somehow, we remain on course. Outside, the silent sky. Partly cloudy.

Do I want to die in a plane crash? I can think of some good reasons to do so. It would bring more attention to this book. It was as if he knew, the reviewers would say, always eager for a prophet. Instant incineration beats a slow terminal illness, like my mother's, and saves money on things I don't want, like a casket. And who doesn't want to know what instantaneous annihilation feels like? As long as it doesn't hurt. As long as some aspect of "you" can survive it. The g-forces! The violent decoupling of flesh and spirit! One second your body's immobilized against your chair, your face distorted by speed, the next you're a heap of burning ashes! Or something!

But my husband, there in the aisle seat. To imagine him alone in our apartment saddens me even more than the thought of perishing together. He should live longer, though; he's younger. I told him, "Don't be like Colin Firth in *A Single Man*. Don't contemplate suicide. And fuck the hot Spanish hustler who offers you a freebie. Imagine I'm watching." One of those sudden cataclysmic plane crashes wouldn't give us time to mourn, or write *I love you, take care of Ignacio* to our survivors on a napkin. Maybe we could attempt a warp-mouthed goodbye kiss. BAM! Then you guys can do all the mourning. Yes, the living always do all the mourning. No, it's not fair.

"This species of madness,"
Fernando Pessoa

Skinless

Imagine serving a life sentence in a prison you had to love or be accused of hating yourself. So we see the body. So especially we see the skin.

Who are we skinless? Anyone?

Imagine everyone without skin—more naked than nakedness, skeleton teeth chattering into cell phones, striding striated through city landscapes like anatomical illustrations, our bulgy eyeballs swiveled by bacon slices, flexing rotisserie chicken calves. No genitals.

Who will you discriminate against now? The brown-eyed? The diminutive? The squeaky-voiced?

"The wind in the darkness howls," Fernando Pessoa

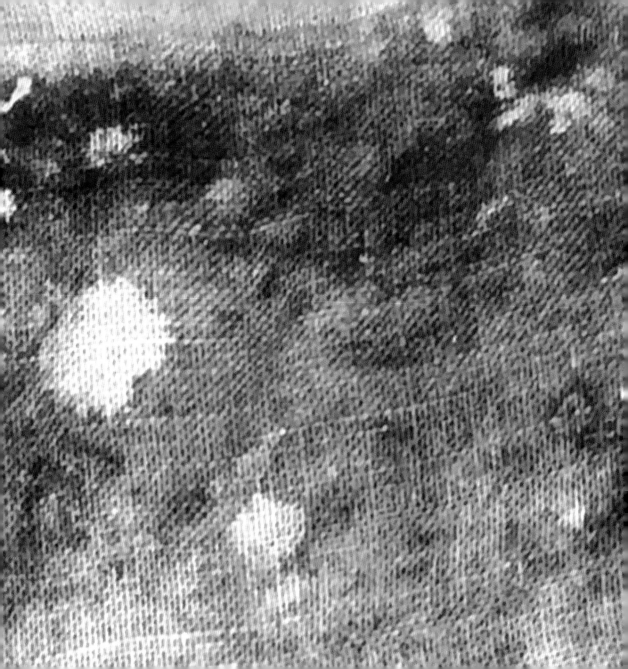

50

51

Rinse Aid

Maybe someone has written a poem that can wash your dishes. Assuming the poet could do such a thing, and that washing dishes provides something more practical (and therefore more desirable) than poetry, which provides . . . What exactly? Bafflement, for most people. For others, a set of ready-made emotional responses? A thing to fear and scorn because its utility is not self-evident? Assuming that a poet could write verse that performs household chores, and could sell his words for that purpose, why would he do anything else? Too much desire for practicality, or the expectation that everything in

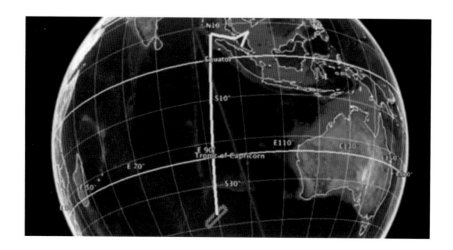

existence must have a practical application, especially one that causes money to fall from the sky, has filled the world with annoying blockheads—boring, frustrating people with no respect for pleasure, intuition, absurdity, beauty, or the many beautiful combinations of those elements, a.k.a. the substance of experience on this planet. Even worse, despite their disrespect for the arts, they love sports, which are far more impractical than art. They go to work every day and hand over their lives to dysfunctional startups that make no practical use of their minds or resources, that cause debilitating types of stress and trauma, but they think artists crazy and self-destructive. Find me a business like a poem—constructed with ecstasy and precision, guided by honesty, truth-seeking, compassionate. I'll work there.

Inward!

You must accept that my identity is whatever I say it is. But the I that I am consists of an ever-changing mystery, a marbled swirl of oily rainbows and pond scum, a combination many-headed hydra, riddling sphinx on Ritalin, and multifoliate Medusa. What I say my identity is might not be what my identity is. I might be in the process of reinventing identity itself. I can say things about my identity that, if you say them, I will deny, and which, if you say them, will offend me, even if true. *Especially* if true. I reserve the right to change my identity before my mouth has finished describing my identity. My identity is a hurricane, calm and empty at the center, outside the eye a category 5, knocking over palm trees, flooding intersections, ripping off tin roofs and decapitating Floridians. If my identity was a kitchen, you would be locked out, while inside, something that smelled exactly like charred bacon burned in a cast-iron skillet. I would also be locked out, but I could tell you with complete certainty that the smell was not bacon, even though I might not know, or want you to know, what it actually was. I could tell you the pot was made of Teflon. I could legitimately say that nothing in there was on fire.

"To travel! To
change countries,"
Fernando Pessoa

The Algorithm

One day, after years of pegging me as a tea drinker, a Vietnam veteran, an Indian teen girl who buys many prune suppositories, a sixty-six-year-old Tongan Baha'i lesbian dentist living on an ashram in Paraguay, the algorithm suddenly got me. It showed me things both desirable and affordable—a bag of peanuts, a mechanical pencil, a haircut by a talented barber-in-training. It had access to my budget, my annual income, and the dates of my paychecks. So on days when I felt flush, it would show me photographs of presents that seemed perfect for my spouse: certain sweaters, a juicer, a paper shredder, running shoes. It linked itself to my schedule and accurately predicted not only which dates I would travel, but by which method, and if by air, on which airline. It knew of my preference for archipelagoes, and former colonies with great literature.

On business trips, it sometimes surmised that I would want to spend a couple of extra days in a particular city with a friend for whom I had a special fondness. It always suggested the more egalitarian (though slightly more expensive) airline, which also had more legroom, because it knew I had a disdain for dividing people by social class and it knew I was taller than average. It also picked potential seats toward the back of the plane, knowing that I preferred them because of a story I had read long ago in a children's book that belonged to my sister, called *Strange but True*. The story concerned a flight attendant who fell 33,330 feet after a bomb destroyed her plane, and explained that she had survived in part because she had been in the tail end of the fuselage, which had fallen intact into a deep, cushioning snowbank. If I accidentally forgot to book a night at a hotel during a trip, the algorithm always corrected this error just before I noticed. The algorithm could tell whether I wanted to buy a weekly MetroCard, a monthly one, or one that debited cash based on which day of the week the current one would expire and what I intended to do over the weekend.

After a while, the algorithm could predict when I would go to the supermarket (the store was near my workplace and I sometimes—but not always—stopped there on the way home) and which items I would purchase, and it would send my order ahead of time, so that when I arrived, a shopping bag full not just of the items I usually purchased, but of things I would have bought on impulse, awaited me. It accurately predicted which items I would select from the salad bar, and at what quantities, and would send this information to the store ahead of time so that a clerk could assemble my order in a recyclable box. I would peer into my shopping bag and the box to make sure that the algorithm had not made any mistakes. It never did.

Later on, it began to speak for me, saying the sorts of things that I would love to have articulated but which usually remained hazy subconscious questions. It told the people I loved that I loved them, explained my negative feelings to those I disliked, and justified my ambivalence to anyone in between. It began engaging my friends with intriguing moral conundrums and recalled hundreds of anecdotes from all areas of my past, things I didn't even remember myself until it retold them. It could recount the plots of all the books I had read and all the movies I had seen, even Bertolucci's *The Conformist*, which I had seen in a revival at the Castro while jet-lagged and had mostly slept through. The anecdotes ranged from funny and delightful to shameful and excruciating, but they always clarified whatever point I'd meant to make when the algorithm began speaking for me. I now swung through my days in a state of wondrous gratitude.

The algorithm had read everything I'd written, from a picture book about a bird I'd pasted together in third grade, to a story called "The Annoying Dime" from my high school literary magazine, to a multitude of nonsense words I'm in the habit of inventing while playing Scrabble and defining in a ridiculous list, to unpublished scraps of ideas I typed into my phone just a few minutes previously. Soon it graduated from suggesting next words and phrases to proposing paragraphs that I might write merely by pressing OK. These were not mere pastiche or parody; when I read, I always had to admit that the algorithm had captured my essence and style, even when I invented a character's voice, that it knew how I felt, and how I would feel, which subjects excited my imagination, and which words I would put in which order, helping to vault me over the tedious process of rewriting and editing and instead letting me zoom to a few choice sentences, as polished as brass. How generous of it, I thought, how selfless of this algorithm, how well it has studied and known me, almost to have loved me, that it has absorbed me so completely that it can offer up its writing to me *as* me, that it will allow me to use the words it has generated to further my aims, my ambitions, my dreams. In fact it is my writing, for without me, the algorithm would not know what to do; it wouldn't have anything to do! I fully expect that it will continue to write my work long after I am through with this world—I would have it no other way.

The algorithm eventually began to write all of my work, things that I am certain I would have written myself if the algorithm had not predicted so accurately that I would do so. It taught my students and wrote as I enjoyed increased leisure time, during which I would watch television or play tennis, a hobby I had initially taken up as a test, in order to throw the algorithm off—naughty me!—and then for which I was surprised to discover a passion. The algorithm nevertheless predicted both my insincere turn of mind and the sincere one that followed it; it rented time on a tennis court for me one week before I "decided" to play tennis, informing me only after I had made the decision, and followed up by purchasing tennis racquets and shoes a few weeks later with my credit card numbers and PINs, which it has always correctly guessed. Nowadays, I catch myself wondering what I will want to do next, waiting eagerly for it to tell me, to show me to myself.

"This great wavering between."
Fernando Pessoa

?

The high priests of my religion, which has no name and no social structure, walk up the aisles of the church, a church that has no aisles, no pews, a church that has no church. The church-free church has no location, except perhaps here, on this page, in your mind, as you read, disappearing before you can completely perceive it, like a half-seen bird in flight that passes, momentarily reflected in a window you did not look through.

The priests, who have no gender and preach in languages of their own invention, which others may interpret but never understand, and for whom this lack of explanation remains sacred, carry with them, for the congregation to behold in solemnity, a gigantic wooden question mark that glows in the dim light streaming in from small windows above the altar. This punctuation represents all the accepted truths we have not really gathered in this non-place to doubt—to worship doubt; to worship even the doubt of our doubts.

Heehhh

We think we know the heart, but we can't even
    see through the skin.
                    —Sounds Like an Epigraph, But Isn't

"Dreams, systems,
myths, ideals,"
Fernando Pessoa

Patheticality of shining
ambitionousness, albumenically

foreheaded. Displayed mouthteeth
desire thereof, displayed within

Nothing patheticalizes ambitionousness
more albumenically than shining foreheaded

(Pathetical parenthetical) in dust, try
Teeth teeth teeth failure

Face egg intrinsicaculous ideation calculust
Thy thigh, though thou thought ought aught

Aww, a thing that disresembled ugh
Tried tried and faced faded could not communivate
Combustitiative oops

We skunk skulk snuck suck fuck up
Hardantageously not to withstandingleberryl

Um,

not

127

The Death of the Critic

The editors worked meticulously, posthumously, to create a person.

In this process, they found, most joyously, job security for Michel Foucault.

In life, the person had worked to avoid personhood, despite his family name: Person.

If the world teaches you anything, it is that interpretation beats creation.

Wipe the language off everything and what do you have left? Some other planet.

The critics determined what constituted the work. They had the proper training.

They found the most egotistical occupations and planted their flag.

"An artist makes things, but exists less and less."

You are just a vehicle for the invention of a thing that I legitimize by deciphering it.

It figures you are a Gemini, Fernando.

The long-dead man had no recourse; he was a recorpse.

"I divide what I know,"
Fernando Pessoa

The Reason Passing Reason

The reason passing reason:
That all must have a purpose,
From extramarital liaison
To enigmatic phlurphus.

Events merely continue,
Absent all ascendant sense,
No logic did begin you,
Nor will any guide you hence.

MENSAGEM DE ERRO
(ERROR MESSAGE)

Gold

Man wants, invents God, God condones. Good God, Prince Henry put God
in L and struck gold. For the love of Gold. Go to L.

And you, too, Fernando, finally yourself but not
Yourself, praising in various iambs the men who taught Europe it could
discover people. Published at last. Once.

The sea belongs to those with the best weapons. If they say God said it,
God said it, so shut up. Believe. The Lord is my crowbar, the world a treasure
chest filled with posthumous papers. Nothing's Portuguese anymore. Not
Macau. Not even Portugal! The sea spoke back.

Snap. Snap. Snap. The legend said that gold coins fell from African skulls
when struck at a certain precise angle. So many brained, so sloppily, and gold
found

Elsewhere. Well. Few stop at that muddy village called Truth; no, not when
they spot Money City glittering on the horizon.

"Prince Henry
the Navigator,"
Fernando Pessoa

Navigator

Here comes Diogo Cão along the Congo,
About to drop his wonderful padrão.
He says, "Don't tell Ngũgĩ wa Thiong'o,
But all must wear these Portugoggles now!

"You may have thought you could not be discovered,
But that's what happens when by Cão you're sighted.
This land is ours—get used to being othered!
(The way that I'll get used to being knighted.)

"Exciting things will happen in Angola,
Cão means business always when he come.
We'll give you backa everything we stola,
It should take just one half millennium."

These villagers Diogo Cão's deploring
Must marvel at this alabaster phantom.
What's chumminess for them, for him's "exploring,"
What he calls "trade," they'll soon describe as ransom.

"The Stone Pillar,"
Fernando Pessoa

Eu Mostro Monstruosidade

The sea was Portuguese—it did not know that.
I set out on the surf—it's tough to row that!
I didn't think I'd meet a Negro dragon
Who'd circle me three times, thinking to grow fat
Upon my flesh. And did I have the gonads
To challenge such a hardy mythic being?
Or would I tremble like a pallid daisy,
Conquering no lands, and only fleeing?
I answered him (once I had tapped my flagon),
"I am the perfect king, and I am crazy!"

Ferdinand Magellan

Colonizin' folks as you was travelin',
Spreading Christianity's infection.
Tried to fuck with Lapu-Lapu's javelin—
He showed your ass a Mactan vivisection.

"Ferdinand Magellan,"
Fernando Pessoa

Whose Sea?

The sea is salty due to blood and sperm,
Some blood is Portuguese, but subalterns
Hemorrhaged more, and piled up like platelets.
(How many times, I wonder, must we state this?)
The jizz? It still appears on many faces—
Those subjugated by the paler races.

The traders, going AWOL from their families
In search of "spices," acted as they damn pleased.
Abandonment might spread saudade's spores—
Enslavement wiped out nations, started wars.
Was it worth it. One might ask mankind:
How did the soul grow smaller than the mind?

"Portuguese Sea,"
Fernando Pessoa

Pangaea Proxima

Late night on the plane I am watching the planet
The monitor showing the continents morph
The drying of oceans, the gnashing of granite
The sea growing vaster, peninsulas torqued.

Australia's in Asia and tearing its core up
Antarctica takes a Maldivian dive
Africa's smashing and merging with Europe—
(Now that will be interesting should we survive.)

The continents breathing for countless millennia
Indifferent to all of our frivolous cares.
Blown by tectonics like so much pollinia—
There's no real frontier to which humans are heirs.

Acknowledgments

Brendan Moroney

Clarinda Mac Low

Anna Moschovakis

David Groff

Anthony Tognazzini

Andrew May

Viet Thanh Nguyen

Andy Blossom

Aliera Morasch

Christopher & Kathleen Moroney

The Corporation of Yaddo

The MacDowell Colony

The Edward F. Albee Foundation

Andy Hunter

Doug Stewart

Yuka Igarashi

Mensah Demary

Sarah Sze

Kendall Storey

Shout out to the Pratt co-teachers and students who co-taught me into a de facto poetry MFA: Mendi Obadike, Rachel Levitsky, Laura Elrick, Christian Hawkey, Jakob Holden, Sasha Banks, Jenson Leonard. Horizontal pedagogy forever, y'all!

The following works appeared in the following journals in earlier versions:

"Other Deaths," *Makeout Creek*. February 2011.

"River," "Lifestyle Issue," "Slavish Rhythm," "Flash," "Stop," "Felt," "Dear White Woman I Nearly Hit with My Car This Morning," "Dialectic," "The Person in Question," "In Twilight," *Ploughshares*. Summer 2019.

"Future Youth," "Existence of Existence," *The Felt*. Summer 2020.

"Air Disaster," "Glances," *The Yale Review*. Summer 2021.

Image permissions

© Isaac Fitzgerald

JAMES HANNAHAM was born in the Bronx, grew up in Yonkers, New York, and now lives in Brooklyn. His most recent novel, *Delicious Foods*, won the PEN/Faulkner and Hurston/Wright Legacy Awards. His novel *God Says No* was honored by the ALA's Stonewall Book Awards. His short stories have been in *One Story*, *Fence*, *StoryQuarterly*, and *BOMB*; he was for many years a writer for *The Village Voice* and *Salon* and is also a visual and performance artist. He has exhibited text-based visual art at The Center for Emerging Visual Artists and 490 Atlantic. He won Best in Show for the exhibition *Biblio Spectaculum* at Main Street Arts. He teaches at Pratt Institute.